Treasures of
Dei Verbum

Treasures of
Dei Verbum

John M. Redford

alive Publishing
Publisher to the Holy See

alive Publishing

Publisher to the Holy See

First published in 2011 by Alive Publishing Ltd.
Graphic House, 124 City Road, Stoke on Trent ST4 2PH
Tel: +44 (0) 1782 745600. Fax: +44 (0) 1782 745500
www.alivepublishing.co.uk e-mail: booksales@alivepublishing.co.uk

©2011 Alive Publishing
British Library Catalogue-in-Publication Data.
A catalogue record for this book is available from the British Library.

978-1-906278-09-0

Contents

Treasures of
Dei Verbum

It is a great privilege to have lived during the sessions of a General Ecumenical Council of the Church. There have been twenty- one in the whole history of the Catholic Church during the two thousand years of its existence. That means on average one per century; and a Council only lasts on average for about ten years. So the law of averages says that each Christian has a good chance of being alive during one Council of the Church.

But I was even luckier. Not only did I live through all the sessions of the Second Vatican Council, which met from 1961-65. Even more, the Council took place in Rome while I had the great privilege of studying for the priesthood at St.John's Seminary, Wonersh, from 1961-1967, after which I was ordained priest by the Archbishop of Southwark. Studying theology was unbelievably exciting at that time. We were receiving weekly reports of the Council not only in the Catholic papers but also in the national press. What a change from our somewhat dry old Latin textbooks!

INTRODUCTION

And the most controversial of all the documents of the Second Vatican Council was the one we are looking at together now, the Dogmatic Constitution on Divine Revelation *Dei Verbum* (the Word of God). This document went through five drafts before finally being approved unanimously by the whole Council in 1965. The first draft appeared during the early stages of the sessions of the Council. The final draft came at the end of the Council. So the Council took the whole time to work on this document, while most of the others went through much more smoothly.

Dei Verbum was indeed controversial! At one stage, Pope John XXIII disbanded the preparatory commission because it was not working satisfactorily and formed another which turned out more successful. We must remember that a General Council is a meeting of all the bishops in the world, whom the Church believes are as a group (a "college") successors of the Twelve Apostles together with Paul the Apostle of the Gentiles.

According to the First Vatican Council, The Pope has authority over the College of Bishops as the successor of Peter, whom Jesus called the Rock; but, although he can exercise his authority in the Council, as he did in this case, the final approval to the document of the Council is given by the whole body of bishops in union with the Bishop of Rome. The Pope promulgated the document on November 18th 1965 (by which time I was almost a deacon!). But it was a document issued by the whole body of bishops of the Catholic Church in solemn assembly after much sweat and toil. Nothing could be more important for all of us, saving the Scriptures themselves, as a statement of faith for the twentieth century and beyond.

PREFACE

1. Hearing the word of God with reverence and proclaiming it with faith, the sacred synod takes its direction from these words of St. John: "We announce to you the eternal life which dwelt with the Father and was made visible to us. What we have seen and heard we announce to you, so that you may have fellowship with us and our common fellowship be with the Father and His Son Jesus Christ" (1 John 1:2-3). Therefore, following in the footsteps of the Council of Trent and of the First Vatican Council, this present council wishes to set forth authentic doctrine on divine revelation and how it is handed on, so that by hearing the message of salvation the whole world may believe, by believing it may hope, and by hoping it may love. (1)

*I*n accordance with a long tradition of the Church, Popes and Councils name an important document from the first two or three words of that document. Those words indicate what the document is about. So, *Evangelium Vitae* (the Gospel of Life) was issued by Pope John Paul II on the subject of the infinite value of human life in the face of threats to human life in the modern world such as euthanasia. *Gaudium et Spes* (Joy and Hope) was another document issued by Vatican II on the subject of the Christian living in the world today.

In the same way, *Dei Verbum* ("The Word of God") names the subject of this document, the word which God addressed to us throughout four thousand years, two thousand years before the coming of Christ (the Old Testament), until God's final word in the Incarnation of Jesus the Word become flesh (The New Testament).

It is important for us Catholics to realise that The Word of God does not refer to the Bible alone, but also to the living Tradition in the Church. That is why in the Preface the Council Fathers immediately refer to the Council of Trent, summoned by the Pope in 1545. The Council of Trent defined against Protestantism that not only the Bible is the source of our faith. The revelation of God is contained also in the living Tradition of the Church, such as in the Sacraments, and in doctrines always taught by the Church but not necessarily clearly in scripture. Thus, Trent declared, the Word of God "is contained in written books and in unwritten traditions". We will later see much more clearly what this means.

> It is important for us Catholics to realise that The Word of God does not refer to the Bible alone, but also to the living Tradition in the Church.

What this document is about is often referred to as the Theology of Revelation. "Revelation" means "to uncover", "to remove a veil"

What this document is about is often referred to as the Theology of Revelation. "Revelation" means "to uncover", "to remove a veil". The Church insists, as we shall see, that some truth about God, such as his existence, can be known by human reason; but some truth about God can be known only if God reveals that truth explicitly, as he did above all when Christ came to live and die for our salvation. Thus the Council Fathers refer back to the First Vatican Council, which met in 1870 with the growing threat of secularism. Against the view that the human person can know all that can be known through science, the Fathers of the First Vatican Council insisted that there are some truths which can be only known if God reveals them to us; however clever we human beings become with our telescopes and computers!

But the Church's knowledge about God through scripture and tradition is not static, but grows and develops through the centuries. The bishops of the Second Vatican Council saw the need to place more emphasis on the goal of divine revelation. This is not just to communicate abstract truths, although that is important. The whole point of divine revelation is to give us all a share in the divine life, fellowship, communion (in the Greek of the New Testament *koinónia*) with God the Father through Jesus the Son and in the Holy Spirit. That is the good news we have to give to the world.

CHAPTER I

2. In His goodness and wisdom God chose to reveal Himself and to make known to us the hidden purpose of His will (see Eph. 1:9) by which through Christ, the Word made flesh, man might in the Holy Spirit have access to the Father and come to share in the divine nature (see Eph. 2:18; 2 Peter 1:4). Through this revelation, therefore, the invisible God (see Col. 1;15, 1 Tim. 1:17) out of the abundance of His love speaks to men as friends (see Ex. 33:11; John 15:14-15) and lives among them (see Bar. 3:38), so that He may invite and take them into fellowship with Himself. This plan of revelation is realized by deeds and words having an inner unity: the deeds wrought by God in the history of salvation manifest and confirm the teaching and realities signified by the words, while the words proclaim the deeds and clarify the mystery contained in them. By this revelation then, the deepest truth about God and the salvation of man shines out for our sake in Christ, who is both the mediator and the fullness of all revelation. (2)

Chapter 1 of *Dei Verbum* continues the theme of the whole aim and goal of divine revelation, which is to make us sharers in the divine nature. What an amazing idea! What an idea to make life worth living! St.Athanasius, the great defender of the divinity of Christ, said that God became man in order that man might become divine.

> God became man in order that man might become divine.
>
> (St Athanasius)

In fact, you could even translate what Athanasius said as "God became man in order that man might become God". This is over the top in the sense that we are not God by nature, but only by adoption as sons and daughters of God. Only Christ himself is the Son of God by nature. But sometimes we almost need to exaggerate in order to get a point across. In Western theology, we tend to emphasise the fact that Christ came to save us from our sins. Taken to extremes, this is a miserable idea. As Mgr. Ronald Knox the great Catholic author put it, for many people, religion is just a dodge to avoid sin! Rather, in being washed of our sins by the Holy Spirit, the Holy Spirit of love fills us to the depths of our being. The result is that we become friends of God. That too is an amazing thought. Even more amazing is the fact that even the great characters of the Old Testament like Moses are called the friends of God. During the wilderness wanderings, Moses would go into the tent of meeting, where he actually met God. He came out with his face shining from the divine presence. He had been given a divine revelation. He had seen God's "glory".

But how could Moses actually meet God, when the Scriptures and the Church tell us that God is invisible?

Even in revealing himself and his plans to us, God remains a mystery.

As Jesus said to the Samaritan woman, "God is spirit....." Even in revealing himself and his plans to us, God remains a mystery. He fills everything, but he is above and beyond everything.

God revealed himself throughout the Scriptures in what he said to us, and what he did for us, by words and deeds. How then are we to know when it is God speaking and God acting in history? Or when it is not God, but our own imagination, or even the devil deceiving us? This is one of the big problems of the theology of revelation! This is why God took a long time, two thousand years and more, to reveal himself and his plans, culminating in the birth, life, death, and resurrection of Jesus Christ.

Over the course of time, with stages of divine revelation, God's people, in particular through their prophets and their Scriptures developed markers, if you like, indicators which enabled them to judge that God was truly speaking to them. Sometimes it was through miracles and through predictions of the future. God knew everything, so he could tell them what the future would hold! Sometimes, perhaps as time went on more often, God's revelation was evident in their relationship with God as a friend. Friends get to know each other in ways which are difficult to explain!

...the bride is but the friend the bridegroom, which stand- stand-
eth him, rejoiceth
...because of the bride-
voice: this my joy there-
...filled.

...ust increase, but I
...se.

...cometh from above
...he that is of the
...and speaketh of
...hat cometh from
...all.

...he hath seen
...he testifieth;
...eth his testi-

...eceived his
...o his seal

...hath sent
...God: for
...it by

...Son.
...his

z ch. 3:23
z Matt. 28:
18
ch. 1:15
Rom. 9:5
y 1 Cor. 15:
47
z Eph. 1:21
a ch. 15:15
b 2 Cor. 1:
22
1 John 5:
10
c ch. 7:16
d Col. 1:19
e Dan. 7:14
Heb. 2:8
f Hab. 2:4
Rom. 1:
17
g Gal. 3:10
4 Or, take
unto
himself

CHAP. 4
a Gen. 33:
19
Gen. 48:
27
Josh. 24:
32

Joseph.
6 Now Jacob's
Jesus therefore,
with his journey,
well: and it was
hour.

7 There cometh
Să-mā′ri-ă to draw
saith unto her, Give
8 (For his disciple
away unto the city to
9 Then saith the
Să-mā′ri-ă unto him,
that thou, being a J
drink of me, which am
of Să-mā′ri-ă? for
have no dealings with
maritans.

10 Jesus answered a
unto her, If thou knew
gift of God, and who it
saith to thee, Give me to
thou wouldest have ask
him, and he would have
thee living water.

11 The woman saith unto
Sir, thou hast nothing to
with, and the well is deep:
whence then hast thou
living water?

12 Art thou greater than
father Jacob, which gave
the well, and drank the
self, and his
cattle?

3. God, who through the Word creates all things (see John 1:3) and keeps them in existence, gives men an enduring witness to Himself in created realities (see Rom. 1:19-20). Planning to make known the way of heavenly salvation, He went further and from the start manifested Himself to our first parents. Then after their fall His promise of redemption aroused in them the hope of being saved (see Gen. 3:15) and from that time on He ceaselessly kept the human race in His care, to give eternal life to those who perseveringly do good in search of salvation (see Rom. 2:6-7). Then, at the time He had appointed He called Abraham in order to make of him a great nation (see Gen. 12:2). Through the patriarchs, and after them through Moses and the prophets, He taught this people to acknowledge Himself the one living and true God, provident father and just judge, and to wait for the Saviour promised by Him, and in this manner prepared the way for the Gospel down through the centuries.

*T*he Church has always taught that we can come to know of God's existence not only from special revelation from him, but by our own reason. As the *Catechism of the Catholic Church* puts it, God has put into each human heart a desire for him which nothing else can satisfy. In that sense, we are all "religious beings", because we are born with what the Church calls an "immortal soul". As we shall see more clearly later, our minds are able to go beyond mere material things to consider the infinite cause of everything.

But God did not just leave it there, giving us a desire for him only from our existence as human beings. He created the first Man and Woman specifically to be his friends, talking with them in the beautiful Garden he had created for them. The Catechism teaches that the narratives of the Creation and Fall of the First Man and Woman are primitive stories, but they contain essential truth. There is no conflict between genuine science and those accounts.

So we would not have to believe that the serpent in Genesis who tempted Adam and Eve was real. He was an image of the devil! Nor is there a conflict with the theory of evolution. Pope Pius XII made it clear that a Catholic could hold that our bodies might have come from lower animals, provided that it was maintained that our souls were directly created by God.

> God has put into each human heart a desire for him which nothing else can satisfy.

> There were two effects of original sin; the loss of the right relationship with God which Adam and Eve enjoyed, plus "concupiscence", a disordered nature
>
> (St Thomas Aquinas)

The Church prefers the theory of monogenism, that there was a single couple, called Adam and Eve in scripture. Some anthropologists favour this view. But what is important is that what is called by the Church "original sin", the sin of origin, was communicated to us generation after generation, if you like in our genes! The great theologian, St. Thomas Aquinas said that there were two effects of original sin; the loss of the right relationship with God which Adam and Eve enjoyed, plus "concupiscence", a disordered nature. It is not difficult to believe, surely, that sin is a reality in our world, indeed in all of us.

God set out to remedy our disordered nature and restore that relationship. He summoned a wandering nomad Abraham to be the father of God's own family. When the twelve tribes, great grandsons of Abraham, went down into Egypt, God called his own prophet Moses to lead them out of slavery into freedom; by words and deeds! He called this special people to himself, to follow his laws, and to live justly and rightly, worshipping him as the true God. He promised to deliver them, even though they disobeyed him and worshipped idols when they reached the Promised Land to which Moses led them. God promised in the end to resolve the question himself, by coming himself to save us. The great king David, the Lord's Anointed, became the symbol of the Messiah to come. But when that Messiah came, he fulfilled all their expectations and more so.

ong...
er the nations.

ll all the proud
v down;
all bow all who go
dust,
:annot keep himself

rve him;
  of the Lord to the
eration,
iis deliverance to a
unborn,
rought it.

n of David.

D is my shepherd, I
ant;
: lie down in green pas-

eside still waters;[s]
my soul.[t]
in paths of righteous-

ie's sake.

i I walk through the
f the shadow of death,[v]

4 He

who
    what is false,
    and does not sw
5 He will receive b
    LORD,
    and vindication fro
    his salvation.
6 Such is the generatio
    seek him,
    who seek the face
    Jacob.[z]

7 Lift up your heads
    and be lifted up
    that the King of
8 Who is the King
    The LORD, stro
    the LORD, mig
9 Lift up your hea
    and be lifted u
    that the King
    in.
10 Who is this Ki

: Jerome: Heb *thee*   *r* Cn: Heb *they have eaten and*   *s* Heb
paths   *v* Or *the valley of deep darkness*   *w* Or *Only*   *z* Or h
:   *z* Gk Syr: Heb *thy face, O Jacob*
: Compare verse 7: Heb *lift up*
.1: 1 Cor 10.26.   24.4: Mt 5.8.

19

4. Then, after speaking in many and varied ways through the prophets, "now at last in these days God has spoken to us in His Son" (Heb. 1:1-2). For He sent His Son, the eternal Word, who enlightens all men, so that He might dwell among men and tell them of the innermost being of God (see John 1:1-18). Jesus Christ, therefore, the Word made flesh, was sent as "a man to men." (3) He "speaks the words of God" (John 3;34), and completes the work of salvation which His Father gave Him to do (see John 5:36; John 17:4). To see Jesus is to see His Father (John 14:9). For this reason Jesus perfected revelation by fulfilling it through his whole work of making Himself present and manifesting Himself: through His words and deeds, His signs and wonders, but especially through His death and glorious resurrection from the dead and final sending of the Spirit of truth. Moreover He confirmed with divine testimony what revelation proclaimed, that God is with us to free us from the darkness of sin and death, and to raise us up to life eternal.

A s the Catechism tells us, the Christian religion is not first and foremost about a book, however holy, but about a person, Jesus the Word of God the Father. Of course, the Church venerates the Scriptures as the inspired Word of God. And the First Vatican Council decreed that the holy Scriptures contain revelation without error.

But Jesus is even more important than the Scriptures. Jesus himself does not just contain revelation. He is revelation. I am the Way, the Truth and the Life, he told his amazed Jewish hearers. And he said to them: "You search the Scriptures because you think you find in them eternal life. But they testify of me. But you refuse to come to me to have life." (John 5:39-40) The Scriptures only attain their full meaning when they lead us to Christ.

Jesus is our God made visible. In the past two hundred years, since the Enlightenment, a view has prevailed among some scholars that "the historical Jesus" never claimed to be God's definitive revelation to the world. Jesus, it is said, was only a prophet or a Jewish rabbi whom the early Christians, in their faith imagination, elevated to be divine. This scepticism has even attained some media attention through such groups as The Jesus Seminar in the USA.

Both recent popes, John Paul II of blessed memory, and our present Holy Father Benedict XVI, have repudiated this view as unacceptable and against the evidence of the Gospels themselves, which are to be trusted historically, as we shall see more later. Pope John Paul

Jesus is our God made visible.

ll said that, even as a boy, Jesus was aware of a special relationship with God his Father. As he said to his amazed mother when found in the Temple discussing the Law with the scribes: "I must be about my Father's business." (Luke 2:49)

And our present Pope, in his own right the leading theologian in the world today, has written a best-selling book *Jesus of Nazareth* in which he affirms the reliability of the Gospels when they present Jesus as truly divine. Jesus performed miracles by his own divine power, dismissing the terrified demons who leave the possessed screaming out: "We know who you are, the holy one of God." He taught with authority, not quoting other rabbis or prophets, but prefacing his teaching with "I say to you."

He manifested himself to Peter, James and John on the Mountain of Transfiguration showing himself as the glory of God superior to Moses and Elijah, who appeared with him representing the Law and the Prophets. He made claims such as "Before Abraham was, I am" (John 8:58), linking his own being with the voice on the mountain saying to Moses "I am who am" (Exodus 3:14). These claims were not lost on his Jewish hearers, who more than once attempted to stone him for blasphemy, but feared the crowds who might make trouble.

Finally, after his arrest, Jesus answered the high priest's question, "Are you the King of the Jews" with "You have said so. I am (the Son of God). And you will see the Son of Man sitting at the right hand of God and coming on the clouds of heaven." (Mark 14:62). The high priest tore his garments at what he saw as the blasphemy of Jesus, and Jesus was eventually led to Pilate to be crucified.

Jesus finally proved who he was, God become Man, by rising from the dead bodily, his tomb being found empty that first Easter morning. He revealed himself to the disciples, even to doubting Thomas, who said "My Lord and my God." Jesus then returned to his Father in heaven, not to desert us, but to be with us continually through his Spirit, which he poured out on his disciples, and so through them on us, on the Day of Pentecost.

> *"The Christian dispensation, therefore, as the new and definitive covenant, will never pass away and we now await no further new public revelation before the glorious manifestation of our Lord Jesus Christ (see 1 Tim. 6:14 and Tit. 2:13)."*

We have to treat this last sentence of paragraph 4 of *Dei Verbum* separately. It concludes that, because Jesus himself is the final revelation of God, and he has now returned to his Father in heaven having completed his work, there is no more revelation until he returns at the end of time.

Theologians used to say "revelation ended with the death of the last apostle". The Bishops of the Second Vatican Council avoided that well-known phrase, perhaps

Jesus finally proved who he was, God become Man, by rising from the dead bodily, his tomb being found empty that first Easter morning.

There is, then, no further "public revelation" after Christ.

because we are not sure when the last apostle died anyway! What is clear is that the earliest witnesses after the apostolic age such as the martyr Bishop Ignatius of Antioch, Bishop Polycarp of Smyrna, and Justin the Martyr, all speak as if referring back to a revelation already given, and to which they are not adding, only explaining. And for this revelation Christians were suffering persecution and ultimately a horrible death, without any complaints, only joy at suffering for Christ! There is, then, no further "public revelation" after Christ. That is why Christians, while having great respect for Moslems who worship the one God, cannot accept the revelation claimed to be given to the prophet Mohammed in the Koran. It came six centuries too late, even though it contains much that is good.

Although there are no more "public revelations", therefore, the Church accepts the possibility that there may be "private revelations", visions and healing miracles given as a special grace by God from time to time as needed. Thus the appearances at Lourdes and Fatima are approved by the Church as helping us to be devoted more to Christ and to his Mother Mary in heaven.

But the Church also warns us against being over-credulous regarding claims of visions, prophecies, and healing miracles. False visions can lead us astray. It is always better to be cautious until a vision has been approved by the Church. If we really want to find out what Jesus is saying to us, we do not have to wait for a vision. We can read the Gospels!

5. *"The obedience of faith"* (Rom. 13:26; see 1:5; 2 Cor 10:5-6) *"is to be given to God who reveals, an obedience by which man commits his whole self freely to God, offering the full submission of intellect and will to God who reveals,"* (4) and freely assenting to the truth revealed by Him. To make this act of faith, the grace of God and the interior help of the Holy Spirit must precede and assist, moving the heart and turning it to God, opening the eyes of the mind and giving *"joy and ease to everyone in assenting to the truth and believing it."* (5) To bring about an ever deeper understanding of revelation the same Holy Spirit constantly brings faith to completion by His gifts.

A voice from the past. This paragraph is mainly a re-presentation of the teaching of the First Vatican Council on faith. The first Chapter of *Dei Verbum,* which we have just looked at, is mainly about God's part in revelation, how he reveals himself in what theologians call "the history of salvation". There is little or nothing about our response as human beings to that revelation. The Bishops of the Second Vatican Council clearly saw the need to fill that gap, but did not feel that it was necessary to add much more to what the First Vatican Council had already stated.

It is always good to remember that the General Councils of the Church do not take place in isolation from each other, but are like runners in a race handing on the baton to the next runner. The first few paragraphs which we have just commented upon, and which deal with the nature of divine revelation, are highly original. The Bishops of the Second Vatican Council decided that they did not need to work on a definition of faith, because they had a good one to hand on from the previous Council!

Towards the end of the nineteenth century, when the First Vatican Council took place, the process of what we now call secularisation was already well under way. Many intellectuals felt that Christianity, in fact all religion, had had its day. It was a myth of the past. The young playwright George Bernard Shaw was of the opinion that the theatre had replaced the Church as the place where enlightenment took place!

> The first Chapter of *Dei Verbum*, which we have just looked at, is mainly about God's part in revelation, how he reveals himself in what theologians call "the history of salvation".

> Faith was not a blind instinct, an evolutionary accident, but truly the Spirit of God working in us.

Charles Darwin had already proposed his theory of the Origin of Species, in which he saw the explanation of evolution as chance mutations. And Karl Marx was already advancing a political theory which saw the political process as the inevitable destruction of the old society, religion being "the opium of the people".

In response, the Bishops of the First Vatican Council insisted that faith was not a blind instinct, an evolutionary accident, but truly the Spirit of God working in us. Faith, Vatican I says, was truly a "supernatural virtue" enabling us to receive God's revelation with obedience, because God himself is the initiator. No one, said St. Paul, could say "Jesus is Lord" unless by the Holy Spirit.

But the Fathers of the Second Vatican Council do not just slavishly quote Vatican I on faith. The last sentence of paragraph 5 refers to our growth in faith, anticipating the next Chapter of *Dei Verbum,* which will discuss the development of tradition in the Church. The Fathers want to tell us at the end of this Chapter that not only the Church as a whole develops in its understanding of revelation but as individual members of the Church in our understanding of what God has given us in revelation and what we have received by the gift of the Holy Spirit.

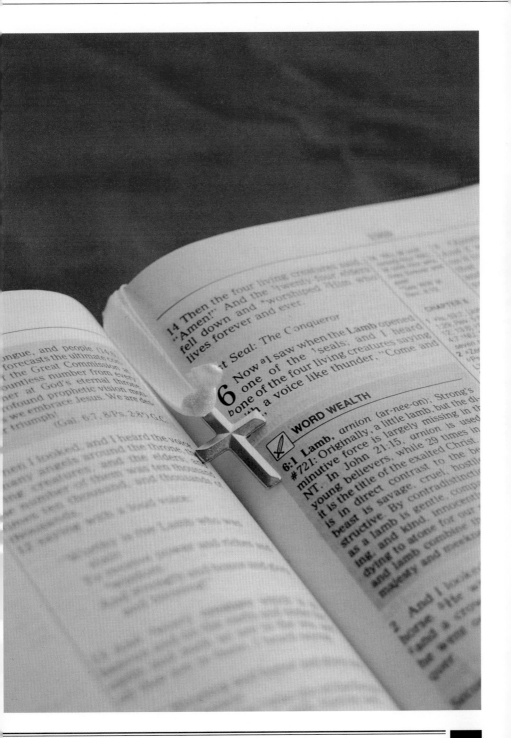

14 Then the four living creatures said, "Amen!" And the *twenty-four elders* fell down and *worshiped Him who lives forever and ever.

First Seal: The Conqueror

6 Now ᵃI saw when the Lamb opened one of the ¹seals; and I heard one of the four living creatures saying ᵇwith a voice like thunder, "Come and

... tongue, and people (14:5)
... forecasts the ultimate
... of the Great Commission
... countless number from every
... together at God's eternal throne
... profound prophetic vision
... we embrace Jesus. We are des...
... triumph!

(Gal. 6:7, 8/Ps. 2:8)

... when I looked, and I heard the voice
... of many angels around the throne
... living creatures, and the elders
... the number of them was ten thousand
... thousands, ten thousands and thousands

WORD WEALTH

6:1 *Lamb*, *arnion* (ar-nee-on); Strong's #721: Originally, a little lamb, but the diminutive force is largely missing in the NT. In John 21:15, *arnion* is used ... young believers, while 29 times in ... it is the title of the exalted Christ. ... is in direct contrast to the be... beast is savage, cruel, hosti... structive. By contradistinctio... as a lamb is gentle, innocent... ing, and kind, innocent... dying to atone for our... and lamb combine th... majesty and meek...

2 And I look... horse, ⁶the w... ⁷and a cro... he went ...
... gave...

6. Through divine revelation, God chose to show forth and communicate Himself and the eternal decisions of His will regarding the salvation of men. That is to say, He chose to share with them those divine treasures which totally transcend the understanding of the human mind. (6)

As a sacred synod has affirmed, God, the beginning and end of all things, can be known with certainty from created reality by the light of human reason (see Rom. 1:20); but teaches that it is through His revelation that those religious truths which are by their nature accessible to human reason can be known by all men with ease, with solid certitude and with no trace of error, even in this present state of the human race. (7)

*J*ust as we saw above in Paragraph 5, so now in Paragraph 6, the Council Fathers are reminding us of the important teaching of Vatican I. That is the "Sacred Synod" to which it is referring. As we ourselves say, there is no sense in reinventing the wheel if the wheel has already been invented!

The teaching of Vatican I is very important still today. That Council asked the question "Is revelation necessary?" It asked the question because, as we have already seen, there were those in the nineteenth century who said that we human beings could do very well without divine revelation, thank you very much. We have science, we have politics, we have money, we have philosophy. What do we need God to reveal himself for?

So Vatican I sets out to answer that question, briefly but very clearly. First of all, the Council Fathers said that we need revelation from God because he wishes to make us his friends, to draw us into fellowship, communion with himself. God can only do that if he tells us some of the secrets of his own mind, which we could not know otherwise. The Church has always taught that we would have no knowledge of the mystery of the Trinity, that God is Father, Son and Spirit, unless God actually revealed those truths to us through the coming of his only-begotten Son Jesus Christ.

So revelation is absolutely necessary if we are to know those truths. They are beyond human reason to work out, inaccessible to human reason alone. But the Council made a subtle distinction here. It affirmed, as

The teaching of Vatican I is very important still today. That Council asked the question "Is revelation necessary?"

> To reach such truths, which should be known to our reason, we need revelation...

we saw above, that there were some truths about God, his existence and the moral law, which can be known by human reason. See for instance the arguments for the existence of God as the First Cause, which we find in the teaching of St. Thomas Aquinas. Aquinas also insisted that we could discover the principle tenets of the moral law because God has written his law in our hearts, as St. Paul said centuries before Aquinas.

However, there is a problem. We have already seen that the human person suffers the consequences of original sin, concupiscence. That affects us even after our baptism. This distorts our reason. This can make us blind to truths which we should know by human reason. For instance, many people today think that there is nothing wrong with adultery, and many people are drawn away to atheism by the propaganda of atheists who attempt to destroy religion in the name of science.

That is why God does not leave us to reason everything out, but gave the Ten Commandments to his people led by Moses, and told them time and time again through his prophets that idolatry was totally wrong, and that they must worship only the one true God. To reach such truths, which should be known to our reason, we need revelation, but in this case revelation is not absolutely, but relatively necessary. Or, as the great Thomas Aquinas put it, necessary for convenience. It is possible to walk from Birmingham to London. But most of us would say, it is necessary to take a train or a bus. Thus God provides important truths of revelation for our convenience. What a wonderful God we have!

CHAPTER II

HANDING ON DIVINE REVELATION
7. In His gracious goodness, God has seen to it that what He had revealed for the salvation of all nations would abide perpetually in its full integrity and be handed on to all generations. Therefore Christ the Lord in whom the full revelation of the supreme God is brought to completion (see Cor. 1:20; 3:13; 4:6), commissioned the Apostles to preach to all men that Gospel which is the source of all saving truth and moral teaching, (1) and to impart to them heavenly gifts. This Gospel had been promised in former times through the prophets, and Christ Himself had fulfilled it and promulgated it with His lips. This commission was faithfully fulfilled by the Apostles who, by their oral preaching, by example, and by observances handed on what they had received from the lips of Christ, from living with Him, and from what He did, or what they had learned through the prompting of the Holy Spirit. The commission was fulfilled, too, by those Apostles and apostolic men who under the inspiration of the same Holy Spirit committed the message of salvation to writing. (2)

J ust as Paragraphs 5 and 6 echo the teaching of a former General Council, Vatican I, so this Paragraph echoes another former Council, the Council of Trent, which took place more than four hundred years ago. But in this case, the Council Fathers do not just wish to repeat the teaching of former Councils which taught important truths about divine Revelation which must not be forgotten. They want to make this Paragraph 7 the starting point of a new and very original treatment of the way in which the Holy Spirit provided for the Gospel message to be faithfully handed on to all future generations until Christ returns in glory.

The Bishops of Vatican II start from the ideas of Trent, Session IV, April 8th, 1546, for two particular reasons. Firstly, they want to reiterate the teaching of that Council, that Jesus Christ himself is the fullness of revelation, and that Jesus gave his revelation not in the form of a book, but to twelve men who were to preach the Gospel to all nations. This was before the four Gospels or any of the letters of Paul or of the early Christians were written. Trent insisted on this point to counter the Protestant view that our faith is founded upon Scripture alone (*sola scriptura*).

Modern critical scholarship has only confirmed this view of Christian revelation being first and foremost "apostolic" rather than "biblical". Modern scholars consider that the earliest written Gospel, Mark's was not finally written until 64 A.D., thirty years or more after the death and resurrection of Christ. And even Paul's letters date only from 50 A.D. onwards. So, for twenty years at

> Jesus Christ himself is the fullness of revelation, and that Jesus gave his revelation not in the form of a book, but to twelve men who were to preach the Gospel to all nations.

> The first books of the New Testament were first and foremost expressions of that living Apostolic Tradition of revelation

least, the first Christians had no New Testament books, yet the Gospel was being preached and lived.

The second reason for the Bishops of Vatican II looking back to the Council of Trent was its use of the word "Gospel", "Good News". Again Trent was tilting at the Reformers, who had used the word "Gospel" as meaning purely the preaching of the Good News of Christ. Protestantism was generally hostile to the idea of the Church having authority to make laws and to decree doctrines. The Protestant image of the Gospel was in general that of the preacher preaching from the Bible alone.

Trent insisted, and Vatican II repeats that insistence, that Christ handed on the totality of revelation which included both "truth and discipline", as Trent put it, or "saving truth and moral teaching" in the terms of *Dei Verbum.* The Gospel meant the whole package of revelation. Even more, Trent wished to emphasise by this, and such is made even more explicit by Vatican II, that the apostles transmitted faithfully this whole teaching of Christ, again before there were any New Testament books written. The first books of the New Testament were first and foremost expressions of that living Apostolic Tradition of revelation which already existed before those books.

JEREMIAH 46

there, shall know whose
tine or theirs.
vou,' says
this
ords
ver-
will
into
hand
ede-
of
his

But in order to keep the Gospel forever whole and alive within the Church, the Apostles left bishops as their successors, "handing over" to them "the authority to teach in their own place."(3) This sacred tradition, therefore, and Sacred Scripture of both the Old and New Testaments are like a mirror in which the pilgrim Church on earth looks at God, from whom she has received everything, until she is brought finally to see Him as He is, face to face (see 1 John 3:2).

8. And so the apostolic preaching, which is expressed in a special way in the inspired books, was to be preserved by an unending succession of preachers until the end of time. Therefore the Apostles, handing on what they themselves had received, warn the faithful to hold fast to the traditions which they have learned either by word of mouth or by letter (see 2 Thess. 2:15), and to fight in defence of the faith handed on once and for all (see Jude 1:3). (4) Now what was handed on by the Apostles includes everything which contributes toward the holiness of life and increase in faith of the peoples of God; and so the Church, in her teaching, life and worship, perpetuates and hands on to all generations all that she herself is, all that she believes.

As it began, so it continued. This is the way in which the Church continued to grow after the apostles died and went to their eternal reward. The Church continues to be an "apostolic" Church, rather than a "biblical" Church, (with each believer deciding what to believe), because the bishops continue to represent the apostles in their governance of the Church. The bishops are both the guardians of the living tradition and of the Scriptures themselves.

We have already mentioned one of the earliest Fathers of the Church, Ignatius of Antioch, in Syria. Christianity first grew outside of what we now call Israel in the city of Antioch, where, as the Acts of the Apostles tells us, those who followed Jesus as Messiah were first called "Christians". Ignatius was one of its first bishops. He was arrested and was on his way to martyrdom in Rome at the beginning of the second century, when the ink was hardly dry on the Gospels and the other New Testament books.

Ignatius exhorted all the new churches of the Roman empire to remain faithful to their bishop, to the priests who were associated in unity with their bishop, and with the deacons. Ignatius strongly believed that this was the way in which the unity of each local church was to be preserved. That was the will of Christ for his Church, Ignatius insisted. The Church from the beginning was not a democracy, but an episcopacy.

> The bishops are both the guardians of the living tradition and of the Scriptures themselves.

The Church from the beginning was not a democracy, but an episcopacy.

To have a church ruled by bishops is not a perfect church, even if, as Vatican II insists, the bishops have had the assistance of the Holy Spirit in ruling the Church and keeping faithful to the Tradition.

Of course, in exhorting each local church's unity with their bishop, Ignatius was also implicitly exhorting unity with the other bishops in the other local churches. The bishops were themselves obliged to act in unity with their fellow successors of the apostles, in order to preserve the unity of the faith against false doctrine and maintain the discipline of the whole Church.

This is the origin of the idea of the Ecumenical Council. The word *oikumené* means "general, overall", close to the word "catholic, universal". An Ecumenical Council is therefore a General Assembly of the bishops of the world who act as a College together as successors of the apostles, to decide matters affecting the whole Church. Christ said to the apostles "those who hear you hear me". Such Ecumenical Councils gather together with the assistance of the Holy Spirit to deal with any matter related to the "Gospel", which, as we saw above, refers to everything related to divine revelation, saving truth and moral teaching. Or as the rabbis would put it, the *haggaddah,* divine revelation, and the *halakah,* the way you walk, the ethics of the kingdom. All this, after the coming of Christ, is the Good News to be proclaimed and preserved throughout all generations.

"This tradition which comes from the Apostles develops in the Church with the help of the Holy Spirit. (5) For there is a growth in the understanding of the realities and the words which have been handed down. This happens through the contemplation and study made by believers, who treasure these things in their hearts (see Luke, 2:19, 51) through a penetrating understanding of the spiritual realities which they experience, and through the preaching of those who have received through episcopal succession the sure gift of truth. For as the centuries succeed one another, the Church constantly moves forward toward the fullness of divine truth until the words of God reach their complete fulfilment in her.

The words of the holy fathers witness to the presence of this living tradition, whose wealth is poured into the practice and life of the believing and praying Church. Through the same tradition the Church's full canon of the sacred books is known, and the sacred writings themselves are more profoundly understood and unceasingly made active in her; and thus God, who spoke of old, uninterruptedly converses with the bride of His beloved Son; and the Holy Spirit, through whom the living voice of the Gospel resounds in the Church, and through her, in the world, leads unto all truth those who believe and makes the word of Christ dwell abundantly in them (see Col. 3:16)."

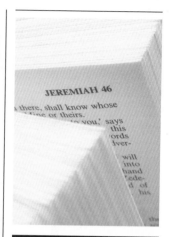

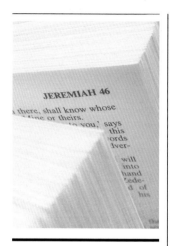

Blessed John Henry Newman, a most distinguished Anglican clergyman already celebrated as a theologian was having problems. He had led the movement which later became known as "Anglo-Catholicism". Seeing his beloved Church of England coming more and more under the power of the State, Newman rediscovered the teaching of the early Fathers of the Church. Many other intelligent Anglicans were following him in his realisation that the Scriptures needed to be interpreted by the living Tradition of the Church.

But where was the Church of England in this Tradition? As Newman examined the history of the early Ecumenical Councils of the Church, he found more and more that those Councils claimed infallibly to know the true teaching handed on from the Apostles. Arius and the other heretics always claimed to have scripture on their side. But the Ecumenical Council of Nicea, for instance, which defined that Jesus was truly God become Man against Arius, claimed to be able to interpret scripture infallibly, whatever the heretics said! Some of the Fathers had even said that heretics had no right to quote scripture, since scripture had to be used within the Tradition of the Church. Even to accept the Scriptures as the Word of God is to follow that Tradition, as we shall see much more clearly later.

Newman came to realise that in order for doctrine to develop according to the mind of Christ, an infallible authority needed to exist, to make decisions, since revelation was, as we have seen, above human reason even if not contrary to it. Newman thought to himself: what kind of church exists today to make such decisions?

Surely not the Church of England, he reasoned, which was obviously quite unable to act with such authority. Only the Catholic Church believed that its bishops were nothing other than those who have received through episcopal succession the sure gift of truth.

The other fact to which Newman's researches led him was to the Bishop of Rome. As the Church's biggest theological crisis, that of deciding who Jesus was, raged for a century and more, the Pope was more and more a source of unity. He was accepted as the successor of the apostle Peter, even in places as far away as Constantinople, the other side of the Mediterranean. At the Council of Chalcedon, which took place in 451, when the papal delegates had spoken, the bishops all replied "Peter has spoken through (Pope) Leo".

Newman, after having written his famous book *The Development of Christian Doctrine,* requested to be received into full communion with the Catholic Church, and lived for two years at our House, which he called *Sancta Maria in Valle,* Mary's Valley, Maryvale.

From his reading of the Fathers, Newman had come to the inevitable conclusion that scripture can only be preserved intact, to develop without corrupting itself, within the Church, and by Church he meant the One, Holy, Catholic, Apostolic and Roman Church. That was the only Church which claimed such authority, and in claiming it, claimed the same infallibility as the Church of the fourth and fifth centuries. And as Newman examined the teachings of the Catholic Church down the centuries, he was able to verify that true development.

> As the church's biggest theological crisis, that of deciding who Jesus was, raged for a century and more, the Pope was more and more a source of unity.

9. Hence there exists a close connection and communication between sacred tradition and Sacred Scripture. For both of them, flowing from the same divine wellspring, in a certain way merge into a unity and tend toward the same end. For Sacred Scripture is the word of God inasmuch as it is consigned to writing under the inspiration of the divine Spirit, while sacred tradition takes the word of God entrusted by Christ the Lord and the Holy Spirit to the Apostles, and hands it on to their successors in its full purity, so that led by the light of the Spirit of truth, they may in proclaiming it preserve this word of God faithfully, explain it, and make it more widely known. Consequently it is not from Sacred Scripture alone that the Church draws her certainty about everything which has been revealed. Therefore both sacred tradition and Sacred Scripture are to be accepted and venerated with the same sense of loyalty and reverence. (6)

*I*t is difficult for any church to claim that its doctrines are based upon Scripture alone. The presence of hundreds of post-Reformation churches all claiming that their teachings are based upon the Bible alone is proof in itself. Each church in fact develops a tradition which interprets the Bible. Protestants themselves are more and more prepared to recognise this fact.

The clearest instance perhaps is that of infant baptism. In the earliest days of the Church, nearly all the converts were adults. It was not until whole communities became Christian that the Church began to baptise large numbers of infants of Christian adults. But where was the biblical warrant for this? In the Acts of the Apostles, we read the story of the miraculous escape from prison of Paul and his companions. When the gaoler was converted, Luke tells us that he was baptised "and all his household". Many have assumed that young children were among their number, but we cannot be sure.

The Catholic Church practised infant baptism because it always believed that from infancy children can receive the grace of God, be cleansed from original sin and become partakers in the divine life. That is, before they are able to make an adult act of faith, because the grace of God will work, as the Church claims, provided there is no obstacle to faith. And the loud crying of an infant at its baptism does not constitute such an obstacle, only sin does, which it cannot commit until it is grown up! That is the testimony of Church tradition.

> The Catholic Church practised infant baptism because it always believed that from infancy children can receive the grace of God, be cleansed from original sin and become partakers in the divine life.

The unity of scripture and tradition as together constituting a single deposit of revelation.

At the Council of Trent there was a debate about this question of scripture and tradition. Some of the bishops at Trent believed that some doctrines had no connection with scripture at all. Tradition on its own was enough. The Fathers at Trent would not agree to the view that some of the truths of revelation were contained in Scripture and some in Tradition. The bishops at Vatican II also wanted to emphasise the unity of scripture and tradition as together constituting a single deposit of revelation. They did not want to say that some doctrines had no connection with scripture. But in saying that it is not from Sacred Scripture alone that the Church draws her certainty about everything which has been revealed, the Council is saying that on the other hand we need the living word of God in tradition in order to understand scripture and for that understanding to develop.

10. Sacred tradition and Sacred Scripture form one sacred deposit of the word of God, committed to the Church. Holding fast to this deposit the entire holy people united with their shepherds remain always steadfast in the teaching of the Apostles, in the common life, in the breaking of the bread and in prayers (see Acts 2, 42, Greek text), so that holding to, practicing and professing the heritage of the faith, it becomes on the part of the bishops and faithful a single common effort. (7)

But the task of authentically interpreting the word of God, whether written or handed on, (8) has been entrusted exclusively to the living teaching office of the Church, (9) whose authority is exercised in the name of Jesus Christ. This teaching office is not above the word of God, but serves it, teaching only what has been handed on, listening to it devoutly, guarding it scrupulously and explaining it faithfully in accord with a divine commission and with the help of the Holy Spirit, it draws from this one deposit of faith everything which it presents for belief as divinely revealed.

It is clear, therefore, that sacred tradition, Sacred Scripture and the teaching authority of the Church, in accord with God's most wise design, are so linked and joined together that one cannot stand without the others, and that all together and each in its own way under the action of the one Holy Spirit contribute effectively to the salvation of souls.

W hat is the "magisterium" of the Church? The word simply means "teaching office". In the Middle Ages it referred to the teaching office of the professor, (usually a priest) who was the *magister,* the "Master" of the class. In modern times, particularly after the controversies of the Reformation, "magisterium" referred more and more to the teaching office of the bishops united with the Pope, the successor of St. Peter.

We saw above how the idea of infallibility was important for the most famous Catholic convert of the nineteenth century, John Henry Newman. He saw infallibility most of all as a gift of the whole body of Catholic bishops enabling them to define doctrine to be believed. Later on, during his lifetime, the First Vatican Council defined that the Pope, the Bishop of Rome, possessed the same gift himself as the whole body of bishops together. Newman was not in favour of this definition, because he thought that it would be misinterpreted by people who thought that the Pope was claiming once more political power which he was losing. But Newman accepted the terms of the definition of the First Vatican Council as a loyal Catholic.

Part of the problem was that the First Vatican Council was cut short by the invading armies of Europe. The Second Vatican Council was able to correct any imbalance in its Dogmatic Constitution on the Church *Lumen Gentium* "The Light of the Nations". *Lumen Gentium* makes it clear first that the usual organ of infallible teaching is that of the General or Ecumenical Council, the whole

"magisterium" referred more and more to the teaching office of the bishops united with the Pope, the successor of St. Peter.

The magisterium is the authentic interpreter of the Word of God in Scripture and in Tradition.

College of Bishops, united with the Pope. Only on rare occasions, does the Pope act on his own by virtue of his office as the Successor of Peter; such as in defining the doctrines of the Immaculate Conception and the Assumption of Mary.

Note that in the Catholic Theology of Revelation the magisterium is not the Word of God, as is Scripture and Tradition. Rather, the magisterium is the authentic interpreter of the Word of God in Scripture and in Tradition. The Holy Spirit gives special assistance to the Bishops of the Church united with the Pope, but the words of the General Council are not the Word of God as Scripture and Tradition are.

Yet, at the same time, *Dei Verbum* teaches that the magisterium is as necessary as are Scripture and Tradition in order for the truth of the faith to remain in the Church. This is verified by the fact noted above, that it is only the Catholic Church which can act with authority to define doctrine and to maintain the moral teaching given by Christ to his apostles. Other churches, other religions, do not have this precious gift which remains with the Catholic Church and with the Catholic Church alone.

CHAPTER III

SACRED SCRIPTURE, ITS INSPIRATION AND DIVINE INTERPRETATION

11. Those divinely revealed realities which are contained and presented in Sacred Scripture have been committed to writing under the inspiration of the Holy Spirit. For holy mother Church, relying on the belief of the Apostles (see John 20:31; 2 Tim. 3:16; 2 Peter 1:19-20, 3:15-16), holds that the books of both the Old and New Testaments in their entirety, with all their parts, are sacred and canonical because written under the inspiration of the Holy Spirit, they have God as their author and have been handed on as such to the Church herself. (1) In composing the sacred books, God chose men and while employed by Him (2) they made use of their powers and abilities, so that with Him acting in them and through them, (3) they, as true authors, consigned to writing everything and only those things which He wanted. (4)

I have described earlier something of the process by which a most distinguished convert from Anglicanism, Cardinal John Henry Newman, through the help of the Holy Spirit made his journey to full reconciliation with the Catholic Church.

Now I will tell you just a little about how a much less distinguished convert began his journey to the Catholic Church; yours truly! I was a boy of sixteen, brought up an Anglican, having just left the choir at church and lapsing. My mother was wise, and without trying to force me to go to church, invited me to go with her and my sister Margaret to a Church of England conference centre called Lee Abbey in Devon, which, I understand, is still flourishing after more than half a century.

At Lee Abbey, I discovered a vibrant Christian community, began reading the letters of St. Paul in the new translation by J.B. Phillips which he called *Letters to Young Churches*, and the apologetics of the great broadcaster C.S. Lewis. At the top of a London bus on my return to begin work at a public library I became aware of God as the source, ground, and final purpose of my being. My life was changed.

At the public library where I worked, I met a colleague who had just become a Catholic. Full of evangelical zeal, I told him of my newfound faith in the Bible. He simply said, "Why do you believe that the Bible is the Word of God?" The only answer I could give which was in any way logical was "The Church, of course". It was the

I became aware of God as the source, ground, and final purpose of my being. My life was changed.

How could you believe that the Bible is the Word of God if there are so many inconsistencies?

Church which gave us the canon of Scripture, the list of sacred books. The Council Fathers quote a few texts of Scripture which name the Scriptures as the Word of God; but why believe those texts? Because they are scripture? But who says they are Scripture? The Church! Karl Barth, the celebrated Protestant theologian, concluded that he could not accept that all the books of the Bible were certainly inspired, otherwise he would be implicitly admitting the existence of an infallible Church.

Eventually I was on my way to accepting that infallible Church, even though that was another seven years down the road. When at Anglican theological college, I found great problems with biblical criticism. How could you believe that the Bible is the Word of God if there are so many inconsistencies? Could you believe with the book of Genesis that the world was created in six days, or that a literal serpent tempted Eve? On the other hand, if you doubted the historicity of Genesis, then would you not throw doubt on the whole of the Bible, including the truth of the Gospels?

It was when I eventually entered a seminary to train to become a Catholic priest that these problems began to be solved. Our scripture Professor, Canon Peter Giffin, a great priest, explained to us that the Scriptures were not only the word of God, they were also the word of human beings who wrote the Scriptures with their own human characteristics, even their own eccentricities. And the Bible was not a book so much as a library of books by different human beings, all nevertheless inspired by the Holy Spirit. Even more, I had the precious guidance f the teaching authority of the Catholic Church in nterpreting the Scriptures.

Vatican I had stated that the sacred Scriptures "contain revelation without error"

> *"Therefore, since everything asserted by the inspired authors or sacred writers must be held to be asserted by the Holy Spirit, it follows that the books of Scripture must be acknowledged as teaching solidly, faithfully and without error that truth which God wanted put into sacred writings (5) for the sake of salvation. Therefore 'all Scripture is divinely inspired and has its use for teaching the truth and refuting error, for reformation of manners and discipline in right living, so that the man who belongs to God may be efficient and equipped for good work of every kind' (2 Tim. 3:16-17, Greek text)."*

n this paragraph the bishops of the Second Vatican Council now come to deal with one of the most difficult problems in the theology of revelation: the inerrancy of scripture. The story goes that, in one of the earlier Councils, bishops were said to have pulled each others' beards when in the heat of a controversy. If the Fathers of the Second Vatican Council did not pull each others' beards over the question of the inerrancy of scripture, that was probably only because so few of the four thousand of them had beards!

As a matter of fact, no previous Council had defined that the Scriptures of the Old and New Testament

The Scriptures are inerrant in their transmission of revelation.

were inerrant. In the face of growing negative criticism about the Bible, the text of Vatican I had stated that the sacred Scriptures "contain revelation without error" *(revelationem sine errore contineant)*. Strictly speaking what Vatican I says is that the Scriptures are inerrant in their transmission of revelation. This was important because at that time there was a discussion about whether revelation from God had become out of date because human science had progressed so far. The Scriptures, the bishops insisted, contain the revelation of God without error and this revelation still is as relevant today as it was when those Scriptures were first written.

The controversy was even raging at the end of the nineteenth century. According to some theologians Cardinal Newman had put his foot in it by apparently saying that the Scriptures were only without error when they dealt with faith or morals. That seemed to be in conformity with what Augustine had said to the effect that "the Scriptures do not tell us about the heavens but about how to get to heaven". But Pope Leo XIII in his encyclical *Providentissimus Deus* repudiated such a view saying that because the Scriptures are truly the Word of God and written by those inspired by the Holy Spirit, those Scriptures contain no error whatsoever.

Vatican II does not say that the truth of the Scriptures is limited to faith and morals; although it is sometimes mistakenly interpreted that way. It does not want to take issue with Pope Leo XIII. What the statement about inerrancy says is that the Scriptures contain no error in that they say exactly and no more what God wanted to say for our salvation. We cannot say that with certainty about any other set of writings, even the writings of the saints. This does not limit what the Scriptures say without error to matters of faith and morals alone, since God might have wanted to say some things for our salvation in the Scriptures which are not necessarily matters of faith or morals, such as the date when Jesus was born.

We are dealing here with what God wanted to say, because, as *Dei Verbum* insists, there is a complete conformity between what God wanted to say and what the author actually said. If we say, "There were sixty thousand people watching Manchester United last Saturday", would it be an error if there were actually only 59,999? Of course not, because we only intended to give us an approximate figure. So also when the Gospels tell us that 5,000 people were fed with five loaves and two fishes it would not be an error if there were only 4,999! Again, we can be sure that the evangelists are only giving us an approximate figure. It is a question, as we shall see now, of literary form.

There is a complete conformity between what God wanted to say and what the author actually said.

12. However, since God speaks in Sacred Scripture through men in human fashion, (6) the interpreter of Sacred Scripture, in order to see clearly what God wanted to communicate to us, should carefully investigate what meaning the sacred writers really intended, and what God wanted to manifest by means of their words.

To search out the intention of the sacred writers, attention should be given, among other things, to "literary forms." For truth is set forth and expressed differently in texts which are variously historical, prophetic, poetic, or of other forms of discourse. The interpreter must investigate what meaning the sacred writer intended to express and actually expressed in particular circumstances by using contemporary literary forms in accordance with the situation of his own time and culture. (7) For the correct understanding of what the sacred author wanted to assert, due attention must be paid to the customary and characteristic styles of feeling, speaking and narrating which prevailed at the time of the sacred writer, and to the patterns men normally employed at that period in their everyday dealings with one another. (8)

We must repeat what we said earlier, that the Bible is not so much a book as a library of books. That is why the tradition of the Church generally prefers the expression "the sacred Scriptures" rather than "the holy Bible", because "the sacred Scriptures" more clearly emphasises the diversity of the different books.

For instance, we have already mentioned the early chapters of Genesis. What of the six days of creation? How does that square with theories about the millions of years needed for the world to have evolved? The concept of "literary forms" introduced in this paragraph is an important principle of interpretation. Catholic scholars agree today that the literary form of the first chapter of Genesis is that of theological poetry rather than that of history.

Note that I do not say "myth", because that might insinuate that the story of the creation of the world by God is not true. According to the scholars, this chapter of Genesis was probably written by a priest who lived during the Exile in Babylon. In that period of suffering for God's people, when they lived in a foreign land as prisoners, they encountered different theories of creation; for instance, that the creation of the world was the result of a cosmic battle between the gods. Oh, no, says the writer of the first chapter of Genesis. "God said 'let there be light', and there was light." There was no cosmic battle, because before God pronounced his word and the world was created there was nothing to have a fight!

> The concept of "literary forms" introduced in this paragraph is an important principle of interpretation.

> The creation of the world is expressed not in a scientific formula but in a poetic week.

So, the first Chapter of Genesis expresses a vital truth, the omnipotence of God as sole creator. But that account of the creation of the world is expressed not in a scientific formula but in a poetic week. The seventh day God rests, according to that account. That should tell us that it is not a "scientific" account. Long before the coming of Christ the rabbis realised that God, the creator of the world, did not really rest. As Jesus said, "My Father works, and I work". That should make us realise that the presentation of creation in six days is a popular form, most probably for God's people to be taught by heart the great wonders of creation. Remember that song, "The first day of Christmas my true-love said to me...." etc., etc.!

I have spent particular time over this one example because there are still groups of Christians, no doubt very sincere, who wish to promote the idea of what is called "creationism". The underlying fear of this group of Christians is that if we deny the six days of creation right at the beginning of the Bible, we are undermining the whole of our faith in the Scriptures. But that is where as Catholics we can trust the Church. As we shall see soon, the Church affirms the historicity of the four Gospels, again on the principle of the literary form of the Gospels, while the first chapter of Genesis is, as we have seen, theological poetry. The Scriptures are a coat of many colours, just like Joseph's coat! We also have the guidance of the magisterium of the Church to help us.

> *"But, since Holy Scripture must be read and interpreted in the sacred spirit in which it was written, (9) no less serious attention must be given to the content and unity of the whole of Scripture if the meaning of the sacred texts is to be correctly worked out. The living tradition of the whole Church must be taken into account along with the harmony which exists between elements of the faith. It is the task of exegetes to work according to these rules toward a better understanding and explanation of the meaning of Sacred Scripture, so that through preparatory study the judgment of the Church may mature. For all of what has been said about the way of interpreting Scripture is subject finally to the judgment of the Church, which carries out the divine commission and ministry of guarding and interpreting the word of God. (10)"*

The Holy Spirit works as we read the Bible, and that whatever text we read, God will speak to us in some way or other if we open our hearts to him.

There is a story about a good lady who was told that, if she opened the pages of the Bible at random, she would receive spiritual enlightenment. So the first time she opened the Bible and put her finger on the page, she was shocked to read "Judas went and hanged himself". A little alarmed, she turned the pages again, and put her finger on the page, only to read "Go and do thou likewise". Now really disturbed, she turned the page over again, put her finger on the page, opened her eyes and read "And that which you do, do quickly"!

There is a unity in the whole of the Scriptures which is the plan of God for our salvation.

We have just been considering the very systematic and scientific study of the Scriptures. That is a much surer method of finding out what the Scriptures say to us than using our index finger with our eyes closed! Nevertheless, the good lady was following a principle which is sound in itself; namely, that the Holy Spirit works as we read the Bible, and that whatever text we read, God will speak to us in some way or other if we open our hearts to him.

Even opening the Scriptures at random can work on occasions; as in the case of the great Saint Augustine of Hippo. He was leading an immoral life, to the great sorrow of his mother St. Monica. One day, while taking a stroll in the garden, he opened the Bible at random, and read from St. Paul "Put ye on the Lord Jesus Christ, and make no provision for the flesh, to fulfil the lusts thereof". Augustine was converted, and became a great bishop and theologian.

In this paragraph of *Dei Verbum*, the Bishops of the Second Vatican Council want to insist that, whilst the historical study of the Scriptures is not only acceptable to the Church and in every way to be encouraged, the Church's understanding of what God says to us in the Bible is not limited to the historical method. There exists what has always been understood as the "spiritual sense" of scripture, that meaning which the Holy Spirit gives to us as we read the Bible in a spirit of prayer, asking God to reveal his way daily to us.

It is not always a case of just sticking a finger on the text of the open Bible and hoping for the best. As *Dei Verbum* says, there is a unity in the whole of the Scriptures which is the plan of God for our salvation. The simplest example is that of the Exodus, that great event in the history of God's people, when they were saved from slavery and left Egypt on their way to the Promised Land. As early as in the New Testament, this event was seen in a deeper way, as prophesying a much greater exodus, the death and resurrection of Christ, the ultimate release from slavery.

Furthermore, the Church uses this deeper sense to define more clearly the dogmas of faith, for instance, those of the Immaculate Conception and of the Assumption of the Blessed Virgin. There is no clear scriptural single text which says that Mary was sinless, although there is no evidence that she did sin. There is no sure evidence from scripture that she rose bodily to be immediately with her Son rather than wait for the General Resurrection with the rest of us. The Church believes these doctrines because they have always been believed (tradition) and because they harmonise with the meaning of the whole of scripture that Mary, having been united completely with her Son during his life on earth, would not cease to be intimately united with Him after her passing from this world.

> As early as in the New Testament, this event was seen in a deeper way, as prophesying a much greater exodus, the death and resurrection of Christ, the ultimate release from slavery.

13. In Sacred Scripture, therefore, while the truth and holiness of God always remains intact, the marvellous "condescension" of eternal wisdom is clearly shown, "that we may learn the gentle kindness of God, which words cannot express, and how far He has gone in adapting His language with thoughtful concern for our weak human nature." (11) For the words of God, expressed in human language, have been made like human discourse, just as the word of the eternal Father, when He took to Himself the flesh of human weakness, was in every way made like men.

One of the most famous pictures of Mary is the icon of Our Lady of Perpetual Succour. Mary is holding her Son, the infant Jesus, in her arms. But the baby is looking away from her, up to where he can see the archangels Michael and Gabriel. He is looking in terror; because they are holding the instruments of his Passion – the cross and the nails, the spear which was to pierce his side, the gall which he is offered as he hangs there on the cross.

Christians quite rightly use that picture to ask for Mary's prayers for them, that she may be a source of perpetual help to them in their lives here on earth. But the immediate message of the icon itself is that Mary is comforting her divine Son as he has a baby's nightmare. That is what paragraph 13 of *Dei Verbum* calls the "marvellous condescension" of God. In the Incarnation, the One who was truly God become Man needed his mother's comforting embrace as a tiny baby because he feared his future suffering for us.

In the same way, the same God who loves us stoops so low as to use human language to communicate his Word to us. As *Dei Verbum* now looks at the Old Testament, this "marvellous condescension" of God becomes more and more evident. We have folk tales, adult stories of sexual misdemeanour, beautiful erotic love poetry, a man wrestling with God who has apparently caused him to lose everything, courageous prophets denouncing idolatry, cowardly kings not listening to those prophets, bloody battles won in the name of God, songs of praise and also of reproach to God for not listening to our

> The immediate message of the icon itself is that Mary is comforting her divine Son

> God will one day save his people, cleanse them from their sins, and lead them to a land where they will be happy in their knowledge and love of God and of each other.

prayers and, in the midst of it all, confident hope that God will one day save his people, cleanse them from their sins, and lead them to a land where they will be happy in their knowledge and love of God and of each other.

If we had written the Bible, we would not have written it the way God wrote it. But after all, we are not God. We have not his "marvellous condescension".

CHAPTER IV

THE OLD TESTAMENT

14. In carefully planning and preparing the salvation of the whole human race the God of infinite love, by a special dispensation, chose for Himself a people to whom He would entrust His promises. First He entered into a covenant with Abraham (see Gen. 15:18) and, through Moses, with the people of Israel (see Ex. 24:8). To this people which He had acquired for Himself, He so manifested Himself through words and deeds as the one true and living God that Israel came to know by experience the ways of God with men.

*I*t has taken Christians centuries to try to eradicate anti-Semitism from their thinking. One of the earliest Christian heresies was instigated in the second century by Marcion, who was a Christian at least by name. He said that the God of the Old Testament was not the same God as of the New Testament; and he rejected most of the New Testament because it was written by Jews! In modern times Christian anti-Semitism has been replaced by secular anti-Semitism with horrific consequences, most of all in the Nazi holocaust.

Even the Catholic man of letters Hillaire Belloc said "How odd of God to choose the Jews". Strangely enough, however, the inspired writer of the Book of Deuteronomy might not have disagreed entirely with those sentiments. Modern scholars agree that Deuteronomy consists mainly of sermons attributed to Moses, and handed down, in the spirit of that great prophet. Moses says to the people as they go through the desert towards the promised land:

"Yahweh set his heart on you and chose you not because you were the most numerous of all peoples - for indeed you were the smallest of all - but because he loved you and meant to keep the oath which he swore to your ancestors: that was why Yahweh brought you out with his mighty hand and redeemed you from the place of slave-labour, from the power of Pharaoh king of Egypt. From this you can see that Yahweh your God is the true God, the faithful God who, though he is true to his covenant and his faithful love for a thousand

God is the true God, the faithful God

That name for God יהוה is especially holy because it was revealed to Moses on Mount Sinai.

generations as regards those who love him and keep his commandments" [Deuteronomy 7:7-9]....

You will notice that the New Jerusalem Bible uses the term Yahweh for God. Therein hangs a tale! There are two words used frequently in the Old Testament for God. One is Elohim, the generic name for God. (The Moslem religion, its sacred language being Arabic, which is a Semitic language like Hebrew, uses the name Allah for God, which comes from the same root as Elohim.) But the other name for God is what the New Jerusalem Bible calls Yahweh, which was a popular translation of that name of God in the 1950s and 1960s.

The present Pope, Benedict XVI, no longer wishes for us to use the term Yahweh. This is because the Jewish tradition never pronounced the four letters of that sacred name יהוה, YHWH, because they had so much reverence for God. They substituted the Hebrew word for MY LORD, 'ADONAI' whenever they read YHWH. That name for God יהוה is especially holy because it was revealed to Moses on Mount Sinai. When Moses asked God his name God said to Moses I AM WHO AM. Christian tradition has always used the word LORD the thousands of times יהוה appears in the Old Testament.

It is important to realise this, because, among all the ancient peoples of the Near East, God's people the Jews had the right idea about God, who was invisible and who was all-powerful. But there was always the danger that they would lapse into idolatry.

> *"Then too, when God Himself spoke to them through the mouth of the prophets, Israel daily gained a deeper and clearer understanding of His ways and made them more widely known among the nations (see Ps. 21:29; 95:1-3; Is. 2:1-5; Jer. 3:17). The plan of salvation foretold by the sacred authors, recounted and explained by them, is found as the true word of God in the books of the Old Testament: these books, therefore, written under divine inspiration, remain permanently valuable. "For all that was written for our instruction, so that by steadfastness and the encouragement of the Scriptures we might have hope" (Rom. 15:4)."*

The greatest danger to the belief in the true God YHWH revealed to them by Moses came after they entered the Promised Land. They entered a culture which was permeated by the Near Eastern pantheon of gods. When they entered the land of Canaan, Joshua the successor of Moses gave the cruel command to destroy the peoples of the land they conquered, men, women and children. We do not know how far this law of the *herem* (dedicated destruction) was actually carried out. But the motivation was clear. If the people of God lived with the Canaanites, they would share their culture and their idolatry.

When Israel was a child I loved him, and I called my son out of Egypt.

(Hosea 11:1)

They continued to lapse into idolatry for centuries, even after God gave them kings such as David and Solomon. Solomon, even though he was later celebrated as a symbol of wisdom, married foreign wives and with them followed their pagan religion. Much worse still was Ahab, a king who lived after the schism between the ten northern tribes and the two southern tribes based in Jerusalem. Ahab married the wicked Phoenician queen Jezebel, who promoted the god Baal, the god of spring fertility. Although the great prophet Elijah triumphed in an encounter with the prophets of Baal on Mount Carmel, Baal, Ashteroth, Moth and the other Near Eastern gods were still worshipped in local shrines, and quite possibly also in the holy city of Jerusalem itself, with its temple containing the ark of the covenant and the stone tablets of the Ten Commandments given to Moses on Mount Sinai.

The great 8th century prophet Hosea expresses God's love for his people, and at the same time God's sorrow that they were continually falling into idolatry:

Hosea 11:1: 'When Israel was a child I loved him, and I called my son out of Egypt. But the more I called, the further they went away from me; they offered sacrifice to Baal and burnt incense to idols.'

The great prophets of Israel, Isaiah, Jeremiah, Ezekiel, and the twelve 'minor prophets' ('minor' because they are short in length not in importance!) also castigated the people of God because they did not practice justice and mercy to the poor. Baal and the other Near Eastern ods would not have bothered about the poor man, as ong as their priests received the gifts (and these gifts ntailed human sacrifices and sexual perversions) to urry the favour of the gods. Amos another great 8th century prophet thundered against injustice in the very rst chapter of his book:-

YHWH says this: For the three crimes, the four crimes f Israel, I have made my decree and will not relent: ecause they have sold the upright for silver and the oor for a pair of sandals, because they have crushed he heads of the weak into the dust and thrust the rights f the oppressed to one side...'

As *Dei Verbum* says, "these books, therefore, written nder divine inspiration, remain permanently valuable".

15. The principal purpose to which the plan of the old covenant was directed was to prepare for the coming of Christ, the redeemer of all and of the messianic kingdom, to announce this coming by prophecy (see Luke 24:44; John 5:39; 1 Peter 1:10), and to indicate its meaning through various types (see 1 Cor. 10:12). Now the books of the Old Testament, in accordance with the state of mankind before the time of salvation established by Christ, reveal to all men the knowledge of God and of man and the ways in which God, just and merciful, deals with men. These books, though they also contain some things which are incomplete and temporary, nevertheless show us true divine pedagogy. (1) These same books, then, give expression to a lively sense of God, contain a store of sublime teachings about God, sound wisdom about human life, and a wonderful treasury of prayers, and in them the mystery of our salvation is present in a hidden way. Christians should receive them with reverence.

Judges 19:1 "In those days, when there was no king in Israel….." If you want to read the most adult story in the Old Testament, read Judges 19-21. It is almost too revolting to belong in the X certificate sections of a bookshop. An old man, a member of the tribe of Levi, made a journey with his young concubine and spent the night at the town of Gibeah in the land of the tribe of Benjamin. At night, some wicked men came to the house wanting to force sex on the man. In the end, they had sex with his concubine, and she died by the morning. The Levite took his dead concubine home, cut her up into twelve pieces, and summoned the twelve tribes of Israel to avenge this terrible murder. After a long battle, the men of Gibeah were slaughtered by the army of the twelve tribes of Israel, and justice was done.

Why is this horrible story in the Bible? *Dei Verbum* tells us: These books, though they also contain some things which are incomplete and temporary, nevertheless show us true divine pedagogy. God taught his people, a primitive civilisation, through the events of history and led them on to understand more about him and his ways. The time that terrible story took place, about the 11th century B.C., was a time when "Judges", that is tough heroes like Samson, rose up to lead armies to defeat their enemies. But they needed a more permanent type of leadership. The story about the Levite ends: "In those days there was no king in Israel, and everyone did as he saw fit." [Judges 21:5].

God taught his people, a primitive civilisation, through the events of history and led them on to understand more about him and his ways.

> King David, became the symbol of kingship, the Messiah, that is, the "anointed" king.

The only solution was to have a king, especially to defeat the new threat of the Philistines, a cultured but pagan people who had sailed in from the island of Crete to conquer the west coast, making Gaza their capital, and who were ravaging the land. The people clamoured for a king; so the great prophet Samuel first anointed Saul of the tribe of Benjamin, who was a failure, even though he had some success against the Philistines. But the next king anointed by Samuel, King David, became the symbol of kingship, the Messiah, that is, the "anointed" king.

David was by no means perfect. He committed adultery with Bathsheba, the wife of his brave champion, Uriah the Hittite (an emigrant from a race originating in today's Turkey). Then the king sent his champion to certain death in battle. Condemned by the prophet Nathan David repented bitterly, losing his son by Bathsheba. David was a loyal worshipper of the true God YHWH, bringing into Jerusalem the ark of the covenant, the sacred relics of the wilderness wanderings, to establish them in a more permanent location. David established worship in Jerusalem, and started the tradition of psalm singing, a treasury of prayers and songs to God which are perhaps the greatest legacy of the Old Testament and a central part of our Christian liturgy.

The first Jerusalem temple was finally built in the 10th century B.C. by King Solomon, Bathsheba's son. Just as David started the tradition of the psalms to YHWH, so Solomon began the tradition of wisdom. This wisdom tradition finds its expression in the books of Proverbs, of Ecclesiastes the wise if somewhat cynical preacher, of the suffering Job, who wondered where God was in all his affliction, and finally in the late books of Wisdom and Ecclesiasticus Ben Sirach. These bring us to the threshold of the New Testament, which names Christ himself as the Wisdom of God.

16. God, the inspirer and author of both Testaments, wisely arranged that the New Testament be hidden in the Old and the Old be made manifest in the New. (2) For, though Christ established the new covenant in His blood (see Luke 22:20; 1 Cor. 11:25), still the books of the Old Testament with all their parts, caught up into the proclamation of the Gospel, (3) acquire and show forth their full meaning in the New Testament (see Matt. 5:17; Luke 24:27; Rom. 16:25-26; 2 Cor. 14:16) and in turn shed light on it and explain it.

As we saw when looking at Chapter One, revelation in Catholic theology does not consist in a book, but first and foremost in a person, the Word become flesh, Jesus our Lord and Saviour. This means that we read the Scriptures to find Christ himself; and we are never disappointed.

> We read the Scriptures to find Christ himself; and we are never disappointed.

This "Christological" aspect of the Old Testament Scriptures is better understood when we look at the period during and after the Exile to Babylon. The Babylonians, the 6th century B.C. superpower which inhabited present-day Iraq, invaded Jerusalem, conquered it, destroyed the sacred Temple, and carried off the cream of the people of Israel into exile, to live as prisoners in the enormous city of Babylon. All seemed over. God seemed to have punished them for their sins by bringing the nation with its true religion to an end.

But prophets like Jeremiah and Ezekiel gave them new hope. They promised them that, far from their Exile in Babylon being the end of God's people, it was the beginning of a new and renewed Israel. Ezekiel, who lived for most of his life in Babylon, saw the presence of YHWH take off like a helicopter from the ruined Temple in Jerusalem and land on the river Chebar, where the exiled Jews were living. Even more, Ezekiel promised them a new Messiah, to replace the King who had been exiled, and a new land, plus a people cleansed by the Holy Spirit. A prophet in the tradition of Isaiah promised a "Servant of YHWH" who would suffer and die for his people.

A prophet in the tradition of Isaiah promised a "Servant of YHWH" who would suffer and die for his people.

This promise began to be fulfilled when the Jews were sent home from exile in Babylon in 538 B.C. by the Persians who had conquered Babylon. The Temple was rebuilt, the returning Jews abandoned idolatry and worshipped YHWH. No more idols! But they still awaited their Messiah, being ruled first by the Persians, then by the Greeks, and finally by the Romans.

It is wrong to think that the Jews back in Jerusalem were just waiting for a political Messiah to free them from the foreign yoke. They were looking for their freedom as a nation to worship YHWH and to follow his Laws under the rule of their own Messiah. The Maccabees, just before the coming of Christ, were martyred rather than worship idols placed in the Temple by Antiochus Epiphanes, the 2nd century B.C. Greek ruler of Jerusalem. The rule of the Messiah would be both political and religious, we might say "the kingdom of YHWH".

Genesis

1 IN the beginning God created the heaven and the earth.

2 And the earth was without form, and void; and darkness *was* upon the face of the deep. And the Spirit of God moved upon the face of the waters.

3 And God said, Let there be light: and there was light.

4 And God saw the light, that *it was* good: and God divided the light from the darkness.

5 And God called the light Day, and the darkness he called Night. And the evening and the morning were the first day.

6 ¶ And God said, Let there be a firmament in the midst of the waters, and let it divide the waters from the waters.

7 And God made the firmament, and divided the waters which *were* under the firmament from the waters which *were* above the firmament: and it was so.

8 And God called the firmament Heaven. And the evening and the morning were the second day.

9 ¶ And God said, Let the waters under the heaven be gathered together unto one place, and let the dry *land* appear: and it was so.

10 And God called the dry *land* Earth; and the gathering together of the waters called he Seas: and God saw that *it was* good.

11 And God said, Let the earth bring forth grass, the herb yielding seed, *and* the fruit tree yielding fruit after his kind, whose seed *is* in itself, upon the earth: and it was so.

12 And the earth brought forth grass, *and* herb yielding seed after his kind, and the tree yielding fruit, whose seed *was* in itself, after his kind: and God saw that *it was* good.

13 And the evening and the morning were the third day.

14 ¶ And God said, Let there be lights in the firmament of the heaven to divide the day from the night; and let them be for signs, and for seasons, and for days, and years:

15 And let them be for lights in the firmament of the heaven to give light upon the earth: and it was so.

16 And God made two great lights; the greater light to rule the day, and the lesser light to rule the night: *he made* the stars also.

17 And God set them in the firmament of the heaven to give light upon the earth.

18 ni
n

22 And God blessed them, saying, Be fruitful, and multiply, and fill the waters in the seas, and let fowl multiply in the earth.

23 And the evening and the morning were the fifth day.

24 ¶ And God said, Let the earth bring forth the living creature after his kind, cattle, and creeping thing, and beast of the earth after his kind: and it was so.

25 And God made the beast of the earth after his kind, and cattle after their kind, and every thing that creepeth upon the earth after his kind: and God saw that *it was* good.

26 ¶ And God said, Let us make man in our image, after our likeness: and let them have dominion over the fish of the sea, and over the fowl of the air, and over the cattle, and over all the earth, and over every creeping thing that creepeth upon the earth.

27 So God created man in his *own* image, in the image of God created he him; male and female created he them.

28 And God blessed them, and God said unto them, Be fruitful, and multiply, and replenish the earth, and subdue it: and have dominion over the fish of the sea, and over the fowl of the air, and over every living thing that moveth upon the earth.

29 ¶ And God said, Behold, I have given you every herb bearing seed, which *is* upon the face of all the earth, and every tree, in the which *is* the fruit of a tree yielding seed; to you it shall be for meat.

30 And to every beast of the earth, and to every fowl of the air, and to every thing that creepeth upon the earth, wherein *there is* life, *I have given* every green herb for meat: and it was so.

31 And God saw every thing that he had made, and, behold, *it was* very good. And the evening and the morning were the sixth day.

2 THUS the heavens and the earth were finished, and all the host of them.

2 And on the seventh day God ended his work which he had made; and he rested on the seventh day from all his work which he had made.

3 And God blessed the seventh day, and sanctified it: because that in it he had rested

CHAPTER V

THE NEW TESTAMENT

17. The word of God, which is the power of God for the salvation of all who believe (see Rom. 1:16), is set forth and shows its power in a most excellent way in the writings of the New Testament. For when the fullness of time arrived (see Gal. 4:4), the Word was made flesh and dwelt among us in His fullness of graces and truth (see John 1:14). Christ established the kingdom of God on earth, manifested His Father and Himself by deeds and words, and completed His work by His death, resurrection and glorious Ascension and by the sending of the Holy Spirit. Having been lifted up from the earth, He draws all men to Himself (see John 12:32, Greek text), He who alone has the words of eternal life (see John 6:68). This mystery had not been manifested to other generations as it was now revealed to His holy Apostles and prophets in the Holy Spirit (see Eph. 3:4-6, Greek text), so that they might preach the Gospel, stir up faith in Jesus, Christ and Lord, and gather together the Church. Now the writings of the New Testament stand as a perpetual and divine witness to these realities.

W e usually think of the New Testament and the Old Testament as two collections of books, the Old Testament constituting a much bigger collection! But in the Scriptures themselves, the Old Testament and the New Testament refer to covenant events. The covenant event of the Old Testament is the covenant given to Moses on the holy mountain with its laws and directions to guide the people to the promised land. The covenant event of the New Testament is the coming of our Lord Jesus Christ to be born of a virgin, preach the kingdom of God, perform miracles, manifest himself as God become Man, die on the cross for our salvation, rise again from the dead bodily and pour out his Spirit on those who believe.

The Letter to the Hebrews is the first New Testament document which refers to Jesus Christ as the High Priest. In the wonderful vision of this letter, the writer sees Jesus as making the new covenant through his blood shed once for all on the cross. By his resurrection from the dead he tore down the veil of the Temple, and his risen body has now entered the Holy of Holies, heaven itself, and it is to heaven that he leads us to offer the perfect worship with him to God the Father.

Jesus himself referred to the New Testament. This was a reference not to a book, but to the chalice at the Last Supper, which was to be the New Testament or Covenant in his blood. The books of the New Testament, the four Gospels, the letters of Paul, James, Peter, John and Jude, and the Book of Revelation are of course very important, the inspired word of God. But their value,

> The covenant event of the Old Testament is the covenant given to Moses... The covenant event of the New Testament is the coming of our Lord Jesus Christ.

> The books of the New Testament grew up out of the needs of the Church in those early days.

as *Dei Verbum* tells us, is as the prime witness to the wonderful realities of the coming of Jesus our Saviour.

As we have noted before when discussing the transmission of divine revelation, the Christ-event and the manifestation of the Church at the coming of the Holy Spirit took place before there were any written books of the New Testament. The first Christians perceived the "realities" of the New Covenant in their life as a communion, a *koinónia*. As the Acts of the Apostles tells us, immediately after the first preaching of Peter, when three thousand converts were made, those first Christians "continued steadfastly in the apostles doctrine and fellowship, in the breaking of bread, and in prayers." [Acts 2:42].

All the essential elements of the life of the Church therefore were present from the beginning by the power of the Spirit which all those first Christians received in their baptism. The books of the New Testament grew up out of the needs of the Church in those early days. The letters of Paul came first, responding to situations arising among the Christian communities he had founded. Then came the Gospels. It is quite credible that what Acts refers to as "the teaching of the apostles" was fairly soon put down in writing in order to transmit faithfully the early catechesis from Jesus' own words. But according to the scholars, it was a generation after Christ's ascension before the Gospels began to exist in the form we know them now.

18. It is common knowledge that among all the Scriptures, even those of the New Testament, the Gospels have a special preeminence, and rightly so, for they are the principal witness for the life and teaching of the incarnate Word, our saviour.

The Church has always and everywhere held and continues to hold that the four Gospels are of apostolic origin. For what the Apostles preached in fulfilment of the commission of Christ, afterwards they themselves and apostolic men, under the inspiration of the divine Spirit, handed on to us in writing: the foundation of faith, namely, the fourfold Gospel, according to Matthew, Mark, Luke and John. (1)

We have already seen that our faith is apostolic, namely, that it comes from the apostles and their associates. They proclaimed the Word, first to the Jews in Jerusalem, and then, with the conversion of St. Paul, they went to the whole of the known world. As the apostolic age came to an end, the apostolic Church saw the need to hand on the message of Christ in a more permanent form.

Above all, they needed to hand on the words and deeds of Jesus himself when he lived on earth. So they composed the four Gospels, under the inspiration of the Holy Spirit. These Gospels would have to be the most important writings for those first Christians, because their faith, as we have said time and time again, was in a person, Jesus Christ, who lived on earth, preached, performed miracles, died and rose again for their salvation. Future generations would have to know his words and deeds in order to love him and to be filled with his Spirit.

As far as scholars can judge, the Gospels of Matthew, Mark and Luke were written first, some time between 64-90 A.D. St. John's Gospel is usually considered to have been written last, at the end of the first century when, according to the tradition of the Fathers, John went to Ephesus to live with Mary the mother of Jesus, whom her Son had entrusted to his care. The scholars have demonstrated that the four Gospels could not have been written later than this. Thus they all come from the apostolic age; as *Dei Verbum* tells us, the Church asserts their apostolic origin.

They all come from the apostolic age; as *Dei Verbum* tells us, the church asserts their apostolic origin.

> "These things are recorded so that you may believe that Jesus is the Christ, the Son of God, and that believing this you may have life through his name"

What Luke, the companion of St.Paul, wrote at the beginning of his Gospel, the third, applies in its way to all four Gospels:-

"Seeing that many others have undertaken to draw up accounts of the events that have reached their fulfilment among us, as these were handed down to us by those who from the outset were eyewitnesses and ministers of the word, I in my turn, after carefully going over the whole story from the beginning, have decided to write an ordered account for you, Theophilus, so that your Excellency may learn how well founded the teaching is that you have received."

Matthew's is the Jewish Gospel, setting out the Constitution of the Kingdom with Jesus as the new Moses; Mark's short and punchy account narrates Jesus Son of God as the Destroyer of the kingdom of Satan; Luke tells us of Jesus as the Good Samaritan loving and forgiving us, whoever we are, Theophilus the patrician or the good thief on the cross; and John the beloved disciple brings us to the summit of the message of the Gospel that Jesus is truly the Word become flesh. As John tells us, "These things are recorded so that you may believe that Jesus is the Christ, the Son of God and that believing this you may have life through his name" [John 20:23].

ninum den ... ... auß ... auß
grau begauberisten ... procediren
... ... 10 ß

den 20 Septembris wider einen terminum auß ihren begauberisten den
procediren ... ... 10 ß.
den 25 Septemb. die begenfrage
auß die b. klagten ... ... 10 ß
ibo den terminum ... ...
... die b. klagten mit ihren ...
... procediren sollen ... ... 10 ß.
den 2 October den forsten terminum
... ... proce-
diren ... ... 10 ß
den 4 Octob. die begenfrage auß
den b. klagten ... ... 10 ß.
den terminum ... 33
... procedirt ... 10 ß
den 9 Octobr. wider einen termi-
... den b. klagten ... procediren ... 10 ß
den 16 October wider einen terminu
... ... die pro-
ediren ... ... 10 ß.
den 23 Octob. das forst ... einen
... ... 8 ß.
die ladung ... ... 8 ß.
den 1 Novemb. den terminum
... ihren begauberisten die procediren 10 ß.
den 6 Novemb. den terminum auß
grau beristen die procediren ... 10 ß.
den 13 Novemb. die b. klagten ...
die gülte ... ... 10 ß.
den 4 Decemb. die b. klagten die
gülte ... zu laden ... ... mal ... 6 ß.
die ladung ... ... 6 ß.
den 6 Decemb. die b. klagten zu lad.
... gülte ... zum andern mal ... 6 ß.
die ladung ... ... 6 ß.
den 11 Decemb. die b. klagten zu
... zur gülte ... zum 3 mal ... 6 ß.
die ladung ... ... 6 ß.
den 17 Decemb. die drei b. klag.
zu laden ... gülte ... schriftle.
... ladung 5 ß ... 15 ß.
den ... ... ladung
... forst ... ... 10 ß ... 10 ß.
den 18 Decemb. die begenfrage
auß die b. klagten ... ... 10 ß
... ...
b. klagtes von ihren begauberisten

... die b. klagten ... zu ... ...
... gestellen sollen ... ... 10 ß

Anno 1608. Den 3 Januarij.

Da ab ... die b. klagt von ihren
... den ... ... zu
... ... 10 ß

Den 15 Januarij die b. klagten
zur Conclusion zu laden zum
ersten mal ... ... 6 ß
dito die ladung zu ... ... 6 ß
Den 17 Januarij die forst zur
Conclusion zu laden zum 2 mal ... 6 ß
die ladung ... ... 6 ß
Den 22 Januarij die b. klagten
zum abschied zu laden zum 3 mal ... 6 ß
die ladung ... ... 6 ß
Den 24 Januarij die forst zur
Conclusion zu laden zum 4 mal ... 6 ß
die ladung auf ... die laden ... ... 4 ß
... b. klagten ... die gült ...
... ... 10 ß
Den 29 Januarij wider einen
terminum den ... b. klagten
auß ... ... 20 ß
... den andern b. klagten die
ladung ... ... ß
Den 4 Februarij den einen b.
klagten zu laden ... alleg ... 5 ß
Den ... die ladung ... forst
zu 10
Den 5 Februarij wider den forsten
einen terminum auß ... zu concludiren 10
Den 26 Februarij b. klagten einen
terminum auß ... zu ...
zu Concludiren ... ... 10 ß
... andern begeren zu Conclusion
zu laden ... ... 4 ß
... ladung ... ... 4 ß
Den 28 Februarij die Conclusion
... ... 10 ß
Den 23 Septemb. die forst zu lad
zur Conclusion zum ersten mal ... 6 ß
die ladung ... ... 6 ß
Den 7 October das forst zu lad
zur Conclusion zum 2 mal ... 6 ß
die ladung ... ... 6 ß
Den 14 October das forst zu lad

19. Holy Mother Church has firmly and with absolute constancy held, and continues to hold, that the four Gospels just named, whose historical character the Church unhesitatingly asserts, faithfully hand on what Jesus Christ, while living among men, really did and taught for their eternal salvation until the day He was taken up into heaven (see Acts 1:1). Indeed, after the Ascension of the Lord the Apostles handed on to their hearers what He had said and done. This they did with that clearer understanding which they enjoyed (3) after they had been instructed by the glorious events of Christ's life and taught by the light of the Spirit of truth. (2) The sacred authors wrote the four Gospels, selecting some things from the many which had been handed on by word of mouth or in writing, reducing some of them to a synthesis, explaining some things in view of the situation of their churches and preserving the form of proclamation but always in such fashion that they told us the honest truth about Jesus.(4) For their intention in writing was that either from their own memory and recollections, or from the witness of those who "themselves from the beginning were eyewitnesses and ministers of the Word" we might know "the truth" concerning those matters about which we have been instructed (see Luke 1:2-4).

*T*here is an old Greek myth of two dangerous rocks called Scylla and Charybdis. Unless ships sailed between them, they would sink from breaking against one or the other.

It is like that regarding the Gospels. Christians can easily become disturbed because they might have held the view that the four Gospels are like tape-recordings, registering exactly what Jesus said and did while on earth. The Fathers of the Second Vatican Council on the contrary refer to the process of selection, synthesis, and explanation, whereby the stories of Jesus' life were put into final form sometimes in a creative way.

For instance, we do not have to believe that the Sermon on the Mount was given by Jesus on one occasion, copied down from his preaching one afternoon! Most likely, the Sermon on the Mount represents a collection of Jesus' sayings (like the Lord's Prayer) which he in fact gave to his hearers at various times and in different places. We must not break against the Scylla of Fundamentalism!

On the other hand, there are those in the scholarly world, such as the followers of Rudolf Bultmann or those in the media who claim that the Gospels only tell us about the faith of the early Christians, not about the "historical Jesus" at all. In particular, such a view denies the reality of the miracles of Jesus, his virgin birth, and above all his bodily resurrection, considering them to be merely "myths".

Most likely, the Sermon on the Mount represents a collection of Jesus' sayings.

> Our faith therefore has a sure ground in reality, not in the imagination of those first Christians.

The Church completely rejects such a view. The Fathers of the Second Vatican Council insist that the Gospels are substantially historical. Pope Paul VI made sure that a statement asserting the historicity of the four Gospels was inserted into the text. The Gospels do not first and foremost tell us about the faith of the first Christians, but about what Jesus actually said and did before he went up to heaven. Our faith therefore has a sure ground in reality, not in the imagination of those first Christians. Neither then must we break against the Charybdis of Scepticism!

In saying that the Church "unhesitatingly asserts" the historicity of the Gospels, the Council Fathers are expressing confidence that historical research has vindicated and will vindicate the truth of the Gospels. The Church, the Council says, has always held to this and always will hold to this (*tenuit ac tenet*), even after the unprecendented critical questioning of the Four Gospels since the 18th Century quest of the historical Jesus. If you want to find the historical Jesus, read the Gospels. As Pope Benedict says in *Jesus of Nazareth* "I believe that this Jesus – the Jesus of the Gospels - is a historically plausible and convincing figure". Amen to that!

...—the ...on the other side of the ...about—well, he is baptizing ...everyone is going to him." ²⁷To this John replied, "A man can receive only what is given him from heaven. ²⁸You yourselves can testify that I said, 'I am not the Christᵇ but am sent ahead of him.' ²⁹The bride belongs to the bridegroom. The friend who attends the bridegroom waits and listens for him, and is full of joy when he hears the bridegroom's voice. That joy is mine, and it is now complete. ³⁰He must become greater; I must become less.

...the one who comes from ...is above all; the one who is ...earth belongs to the earth ...ks as one from the earth ...who comes from h...

Jesus Talks With a Samaritan Woman

4 The Pharisees heard that Jesus was gaining and baptizing ...disciples tha... ...in fact it w...

20. Besides the four Gospels, the canon of the New Testament also contains the epistles of St. Paul and other apostolic writings, composed under the inspiration of the Holy Spirit, by which, according to the wise plan of God, those matters which concern Christ the Lord are confirmed, His true teaching is more and more fully stated, the saving power of the divine work of Christ is preached, the story is told of the beginnings of the Church and its marvellous growth, and its glorious fulfilment is foretold.

For the Lord Jesus was with His apostles as He had promised (see Matt. 28:20) and sent them the advocate Spirit who would lead them into the fullness of truth (see John 16:13).

Apart from Jesus himself, there is one person, called in the Church "the apostle to the Gentiles", who stands out as the man of the New Testament. I am referring of course to St Paul.

Well over half of the writing of the New Testament is linked with his name and his influence. Luke, the author of the third Gospel and of the Acts of the Apostles, was a constant companion of Paul on his dangerous journeys. It was good fortune that Luke was a physician, with Paul's physical ailments from his beatings and rough journeys, before we even consider his "thorn in the flesh" that he speaks about, whatever it was, no doubt needing constant attention.

There are thirteen letters attributed to St. Paul in the canon of the New Testament; out of only twenty-seven books in all! Church tradition no longer claims that Paul wrote the last of these, the letter to the Hebrews. Perhaps it was written by a disciple of Paul such as Apollos, since the letter is written in a style of Greek thought linked with Alexandria in Egypt.

Eight letters of Paul are certainly by him, the scholars tell us: Romans, 1 and 2 Corinthians, Galatians, Philippians, 1 and 2 Thessalonians, and Philemon. These wonderful letters are perhaps the most life-changing documents in the history of the world. If you do not want to convert to Christ, never read them! Paul has a passion for the faith, which began when he met the risen Christ on the Damascus Road. From then on, Paul gave himself body and soul to the salvation of the world. He worshipped

> Paul has a passion for the faith, which began when he met the risen Christ on the Damascus Road.

Paul needed urgently to develop his theology of the Church as the body of Christ.

Jesus as Lord, *Kurios*, the YHWH of the Old Testament whom he saw as the new principle of life in his baptism in the Spirit, for all time.

Scholars dispute the Pauline authorship of five letters: Ephesians, Colossians, and the "Pastoral Letters" 1 and 2 Timothy and Titus. Certainly those letters bear the spirit of Paul, at least as communicated by his disciples. I personally think that the differences between these later letters of Paul and the early undisputed letters are easily explained, not as a "pseudo-Paul" but as part of the genuine development of his thinking. In particular, the Church was growing throughout the Roman Empire, and Paul needed urgently to develop his theology of the Church as the body of Christ, and to hand on his apostolic authority to pastors who would take his place worthily like Timothy and Titus.

There is little or no time to discuss the letters of Peter, John, James, and Jude. Peter speaks of true worship in Christ, John of true love in Christ; James is a good old practical letter to bring our Christian faith down to earth; and Jude warns us of the wrath to come. Which leaves Revelation. The vision of the Apocolypse may appear terrifying but we are assured that the Lamb and his angels have charge of the Universe and are led to the blissful vision of the New Jerusalem in the final chapter.

CHAPTER VI

SACRED SCRIPTURE IN THE LIFE OF THE CHURCH

21. The Church has always venerated the divine Scriptures just as she venerates the body of the Lord, since, especially in the sacred liturgy, she unceasingly receives and offers to the faithful the bread of life from the table both of God's word and of Christ's body. She has always maintained them, and continues to do so, together with sacred tradition, as the supreme rule of faith, since, as inspired by God and committed once and for all to writing, they impart the word of God Himself without change, and make the voice of the Holy Spirit resound in the words of the prophets and Apostles. Therefore, like the Christian religion itself, all the preaching of the Church must be nourished and regulated by Sacred Scripture. For in the sacred books, the Father who is in heaven meets His children with great love and speaks with them; and the force and power in the word of God is so great that it stands as the support and energy of the Church, the strength of faith for her sons, the food of the soul, the pure and everlasting source of spiritual life. Consequently these words are perfectly applicable to Sacred Scripture: "For the word of God is living and active" (Heb. 4:12) and "it has power to build you up and give you your heritage among all those who are sanctified" (Acts 20:32; see 1 Thess. 2:13).

*F*or many Catholics, this paragraph could initially be quite a surprise, even shocking. It compares the presence of Christ in the Scriptures with the presence of Christ in the Eucharist. It is not unfair to say that Catholics in general have a greater awareness of the Real Presence in the Eucharist than they have in the presence of Christ in the Scriptures, even though they recognise the Scriptures as the Word of God.

The presence of Christ in the Eucharist is unique, even as compared with the Scriptures. Thomas Aquinas, the great theologian of the Eucharist, named it a "substantial" presence; namely, the consecrated bread and wine become in essence the true body and blood of Christ. The books of scripture do not become the substantial presence of Christ in the same way! No, as we have discussed earlier, those books are the Word of God because God says through the human authors of scripture exactly what he wants to say, no more and no less.

But it is precisely in this way that Christ is present in the Scriptures, most of all in the solemn reading of the Gospel. That is why we make the sign of the cross on our foreheads, lips and our heart; praying that the words of the Gospel will be understood by our minds, professed with our lips, and remain in our hearts, being reflected in consequence in our actions.

Thus, in the rhythm of the Mass, the Liturgy of the Word prepares us for the Liturgy of the Eucharist. The feast has two stages. We first hear the Word, listening to what

> Christ is present in the Scriptures, most of all in the solemn reading of the Gospel.

In the rhythm of the Mass, the Liturgy of the Word prepares us for the Liturgy of the Eucharist.

God wants to say to us. We then receive the incarnate Word in eating and drinking the body and blood of Christ.

That is why Vatican II ordered a reform of the lectionary in its very first document, the Constitution on the Sacred Liturgy, *Sacrosanctum Concilium*. The lectionary of the renewed liturgy, which is now celebrated throughout the Western church as the 'ordinary rite' of Mass, is much more complete than the selection of readings which existed in the pre-Vatican II liturgical books.

"In order that believers can be provided with a richer diet of God's Word, the rich heritage of the Bible is to be opened more widely, in such a way that a fuller and more nourishing selection of the Scriptures gets read to the people within a fixed period of years." (SC 51)

In the revised lectionary, the Sunday readings follow a three-year cycle: Matthew is read in Year A, Mark in Year B, Luke in Year C. John's Gospel does not have a year of its own, but since John chapters 7-21 cover just the last six weeks of Jesus' life on earth, this Gospel is read predominantly in Lent and Eastertide as we contemplate the Passion, Death and Resurrection of the Lord Jesus

22. Easy access to Sacred Scripture should be provided for all the Christian faithful. That is why the Church from the very beginning accepted as her own that very ancient Greek translation; of the Old Testament which is called the septuagint; and she has always given a place of honour to other Eastern translations and Latin ones especially the Latin translation known as the vulgate. But since the word of God should be accessible at all times, the Church by her authority and with maternal concern sees to it that suitable and correct translations are made into different languages, especially from the original texts of the sacred books. And should the opportunity arise and the Church authorities approve, if these translations are produced in cooperation with the separated brethren as well, all Christians will be able to use them.

A ll the first Christians were Jews. Peter addressed his first sermon on the Day of Pentecost to the "men of Israel". But soon, as the Gentile mission led by St. Paul progressed phenomenally, the Church became more and more Gentile. After the horrible destruction of Jerusalem by the Romans in AD 70 the Jewish people developed their own defence against what they saw as the new heresy of Christianity. This became what we now call "Rabbinic Judaism". Thus was created the most tragic, and, in a way, the most profound division between Judaism and the Christian faith which emerged from it.

Since Christians did not know Hebrew, the language of the Old Testament, the Church read from what was called the Septuagint Greek translation of the Old Testament. The Septuagint, meaning "the Seventy", was a translation of the Hebrew Old Testament into Greek begun in Alexandria, the capital of Egypt. A large colony of emigrant Jews had formed in Alexandria beginning in the second century BC. Naturally, they spoke mainly Greek, just as Jews in Britain and in the United States speak mainly English.

According to legend, seventy men went into separate booths and all came out with the same translation! Hence the name of the Septuagint, the 'Seventy'. The Church accepted the Septuagint as the canon of holy scripture.

The Septuagint included Old Testament extra books some of which were written in Greek and not in Hebrew:

> The Septuagint, meaning "the Seventy", was a translation of the Hebrew Old Testament into Greek begun in Alexandria, the capital of Egypt.

After the Reformation, for disciplinary reasons, the Catholic Church only allowed translations into different European languages from Jerome's Vulgate.

Wisdom, Ecclesiasticus, 1 and 2 Maccabees, addition to Daniel, Tobit, Judith, additions to Esther, and Baruch The Jewish Council of Jamnia rejected these books chiefly because they were not written in Hebrew; but the Church always used them in the reading of scripture at Mass, and so at the Council of Trent in 1545 those books were solemnly defined as part of the Canon, against the Reformers who followed the Jewish Canon

When large numbers of countries in Western Europe became Catholic, the international language became Latin. In the fourth century the great Jerome, translated the Old Testament from Hebrew into Latin, having learnt Hebrew from a rabbi. He provided a version of the Greek New Testament in Latin. This became the Vulgate or "common" translation for centuries. After the Reformation, for disciplinary reasons, the Catholic Church only allowed translations into different European languages from Jerome's Vulgate.

However, in the second half of the twentieth century, as a result of the ecumenical movement, there have been many translations of the Bible approved by Catholics and Protestants together. Perhaps the most famous is the Revised Standard Version, an American version originally Protestant, but now published with the full approval of the Catholic bishops together with what are now called the "Deutero-Canonical" books, those books of the Septuagint such as Wisdom and Maccabees originally rejected by the Reformers. We trust that in a hopefully visibly reunited Church those books will be found back in the Bible for our separated brethren also!

23. The bride of the incarnate Word, the Church taught by the Holy Spirit, is concerned to move ahead toward a deeper understanding of the Sacred Scriptures so that she may increasingly feed her sons with the divine words. Therefore, she also encourages the study of the holy Fathers of both East and West and of sacred liturgies. Catholic exegetes then and other students of sacred theology, working diligently together and using appropriate means, should devote their energies, under the watchful care of the sacred teaching office of the Church, to an exploration and exposition of the divine writings. This should be so done that as many ministers of the divine word as possible will be able effectively to provide the nourishment of the Scriptures for the people of God, to enlighten their minds, strengthen their wills, and set men's hearts on fire with the love of God. (1) The sacred synod encourages the sons of the Church and Biblical scholars to continue energetically, following the mind of the Church, with the work they have so well begun, with a constant renewal of vigour. (2)

*T*he Fathers of the Church sometimes expounded the Scriptures in a way which we would find strange today. Augustine, for instance, commented on the miracle of the man in John's Gospel Chapter 5 who was 38 years in his infirmity. Why was he thirty-eight years in his infirmity, asked Augustine? Jesus was 40 days in the desert, said the Father of the Church. That is perfection. 38 is two less than 40; and there are two great commandments of God. How was the man defective therefore, asked Augustine? He was 38 years in his infirmity because he failed in those two commandments.

But if the Fathers of the Church are sometimes over-imaginative in their interpretation of Scripture, *Dei Verbum* maintains that they possessed insights into the meaning of scripture which were based upon the tradition and which we need to recover today.

Since the 18th century in particular, the study of the Scriptures has become more scientific. The Church has encouraged such a development. Pope Pius X saw the need for the scientific study of scripture, and founded the Pontifical Biblical Institute, of which your author was a student four decades ago now! It is important for the study of the Scriptures to be critical, and for our priests and lay people to be educated in that method. But, at the same time, the Church wishes us not to be limited to the historical or literal meaning of scripture. Pope Benedict XVI has emphasised this point in his book *Jesus of Nazareth*.

> Since the 18th century in particular, the study of the Scriptures has become more scientific. The Church has encouraged such a development.

> It would be particularly useful in the preparation for homilies to take a text from those readings and explore that text in its catechetical context.

In paragraph 11 of this Council document, the Church encourages us to use the principles of the unity of scripture, the tradition of the Church and the analogy of faith. These principles do not go against the scientific reading of scripture, but constitute a reading of scripture in the mind of the living tradition of the Church.

One way of reading scripture in this way is by referring to the *Catechism of the Catholic Church* (full edition). If you are reading a passage of scripture, such as the letter of James 1:27, you can turn to the index of scripture quotes at the end of the CCC. If you refer in the Index of Citations to James 1:27, (p.628 in my edition of the CCC), it will refer you to 2208. You then turn to paragraph 2208 of the CCC, (in my edition page 477) and you will see that this verse from James is quoted as part of the section on Family and Society.

In this way, you will be led from a simple consideration of the text, that true religion consists in kindness to widows and orphans, to a much wider consideration of the whole Christian doctrine of the human family and of the family of the Church. It sounds complicated, but in fact it is a very simple method, and it can become quite automatic as you practise it frequently. It would be particularly useful in the preparation for homilies to take a text from those readings and explore that text in its catechetical context. In that way, using the CCC together with the Bible, you will often also encounter the interpretations of theologians and the Fathers, which will enrich your understanding of scripture.

24. Sacred theology rests on the written word of God, together with sacred tradition, as its primary and perpetual foundation. By scrutinizing in the light of faith all truth stored up in the mystery of Christ, theology is most powerfully strengthened and constantly rejuvenated by that word. For the Sacred Scriptures contain the word of God and since they are inspired really are the word of God; and so the study of the sacred page is, as it were, the soul of sacred theology. (3) By the same word of Scripture the ministry of the word also, that is, pastoral preaching, catechetics and all Christian instruction, in which the liturgical homily must hold the foremost place, is nourished in a healthy way and flourishes in a holy way.

*T*he last paragraph laid the foundations of the correct interpretation of scripture. This paragraph attempts to lay the foundations of theology.

Dei Verbum has already insisted in Chapter 2, that both scripture and tradition are the Word of God. Thus both scripture and tradition are necessary for theology. But the Council Fathers wanted to insist also that scripture and tradition should not be seen as two separate entities, as Catholic theologians have sometimes viewed them, but as two well-springs from a single source.

This paragraph, in consequence, like others we have seen before in this inspiring document, breaks new ground at this point. It seems to give a certain primacy to scripture, "sacred theology rests on the written Word of God" *(Sacra theologia in verbo Dei.....innititur)*. However, at the same time, it sees scripture as "one with sacred tradition" (*una cum sacra traditione*).

In the first thousand years of the Christian faith, those who taught theology, mainly bishops and their assistants, based their theology on interpreting scripture, particularly in homilies. Their interpretation was based upon and united with the living tradition of the Church.

In the second millennium, with the introduction of Aristotelian philosophy into Europe, a more rationally based approach to theology came into vogue, led by the great Thomas Aquinas. All the Masters of Theology had to interpret the "sacred page" (*sacra pagina*) in lectures,

Both scripture and tradition are necessary for theology.

> New manuscripts of the letters of Paul were discovered in the sands of Egypt only in the last century.

commenting verse by verse on scripture. But after the Sentences (i.e. judgements) of Peter Lombard, more and more theology began to ask questions isolated from the biblical texts. The great systems of theology were produced by the doctors of theology such as Aquinas, Bonaventura, and Scotus. This change came about at the same time as the age of science was dawning in Europe.

The advantage of this approach was that rational problems were directly addressed by theology. That is still necessary. But a shift of emphasis became apparent as successive drafts of *Dei Verbum* were produced. The early drafts were scholastic; but, as revisions came, the whole structure and style of the document became different. It was the fifth draft that was finally accepted in 1965. It moves forward by expounding themes, in order to present the riches of divine revelation, with biblical texts constantly quoted. It attempts to draw out theology from scripture, rather than use scripture simply as a source of proof-texts for dogmatic statements already made.

The primacy of scripture (affirming the primacy of Scripture is not a denial that Sacred Tradition is equally the Word of God) arises from the peculiar nature of the written word. God's word in tradition is often what we call "non-verbal", especially in the liturgy of the Church which is an authoritative expression of living tradition. The special gift of the written word of God is its concrete nature and its permanence. That even includes the superiority of the written word over recorded technology such as computer disks. In a thousand years, will today's computer disks still be compatible? New manuscripts of the letters of Paul were discovered in the sands of Egypt only in the last century. They are two thousand years old, and still can be read!

25. Therefore, all the clergy must hold fast to the Sacred Scriptures through diligent sacred reading and careful study, especially the priests of Christ and others, such as deacons and catechists who are legitimately active in the ministry of the word. This is to be done so that none of them will become "an empty preacher of the word of God outwardly, who is not a listener to it inwardly" (4) since they must share the abundant wealth of the divine word with the faithful committed to them, especially in the sacred liturgy. The sacred synod also earnestly and especially urges all the Christian faithful, especially Religious, to learn by frequent reading of the divine Scriptures the "excellent knowledge of Jesus Christ" (Phil. 3:8). "For ignorance of the Scriptures is ignorance of Christ." (5) Therefore, they should gladly put themselves in touch with the sacred text itself, whether it be through the liturgy, rich in the divine word, or through devotional reading, or through instructions suitable for the purpose and other aids which, in our time, with approval and active support of the shepherds of the Church, are commendably spread everywhere. And let them remember that prayer should accompany the reading of Sacred Scripture, so that God and man may talk together; for "we speak to Him when we pray; we hear Him when we read the divine saying." (6)

*M*y mother, a good Evangelical Anglican, instilled in me from my childhood the importance of reading the Bible daily. Every night, before going to bed, she would read what she called her "portion" from a booklet of daily readings with short notes. At Sunday School I was taught to sing the childrens' chorus: "The best book to read is the Bible, the best book to read is the Bible. If you read it every day, it will help you on your way. Oh, the best book to read is the Bible".

Not the greatest poetry ever written; but I have remembered it after more than seventy years on this earth by the grace of God! Since the Second Vatican Council, many Catholics have begun this practice, helped in particular by *Bible Alive*. We have already mentioned the "richer fare" of the written Word of God provided in the new lectionary. Some friends of mine always read the daily scripture readings from Mass, either in preparation for going to daily Mass, or if they cannot attend Mass, they at least read the First Reading and the Gospel of the day.

The Church teaches that, because the Scriptures are the written word of God, they are superior to any other form of devotional reading; even to the lives of the saints or other spiritual writers such as St. John of the Cross. The Church encourages us to think of the Scriptures, if you like, as our "daily bread", while we might view the lives of the saints or their spiritual writings as a sweet second course!

> The Church teaches that, because the Scriptures are the written word of God, they are superior to any other form of devotional reading.

> We were taught as celibate priests to call the breviary our "wife".
> It is... good practice... for every literate Christian... to read the Bible from cover to cover... with minimal or no notes.

Priests in particular have the obligation to pray the daily office or the "breviary" as their own spiritual daily bread and as part of their priestly duty to pray for the people of God. We were taught as celibate priests to call the breviary our "wife". In fact, an old priest friend of mine and mentor used to say that very often if a priest left the priesthood it was because he had neglected his daily office.

The Divine Office goes back to the first prayers of the Christians, the "prayers" which as pious Jews they said daily in the Temple (Acts 2:42; *Dei Verbum* 10). Those prayers were no doubt the Psalms of David, which eventually became the basis of the monastic office, seven daily services which the monks call the *opus Dei*, the "work of God". More and more lay people now, as well as religious, are being encouraged to use part of this Divine Office as their way of daily scripture reading.

However, one disadvantage of all these methods is that the biblical texts are not seen in their contexts, particularly as complete books. Therefore, since the Second Vatican Council, local bishops, parishes and catechetical institutes have promoted courses on Scripture which outline the content and meaning of both the Old and the New Testament. This systematic presentation of scripture is important not only for young people in schools, but also for the education of adults. It is also a good practice, in my humble opinion, for every literate Christian, once in a lifetime, to read the Bible from cover to cover, from beginning to end, with minimal

r no notes. You will achieve this in about two years, if
ou take a chapter a day!

...read the Bible from cover to cover... You will achieve this in about two years...

"It devolves on sacred bishops "who have the apostolic teaching"(7) to give the faithful entrusted to them suitable instruction in the right use of the divine books, especially the New Testament and above all the Gospels. This can be done through translations of the sacred texts, which are to be provided with the necessary and really adequate explanations so that the children of the Church may safely and profitably become conversant with the Sacred Scriptures and be penetrated with their spirit.

Furthermore, editions of the Sacred Scriptures, provided with suitable footnotes, should be prepared also for the use of non-Christians and adapted to their situation. Both pastors of souls and Christians generally should see to the wise distribution of these in one way or another." (DV25)

26. In this way, therefore, through the reading and study of the sacred books "the word of God may spread rapidly and be glorified" (2 Thess. 3:1) and the treasure of revelation, entrusted to the Church, may more and more fill the hearts of men. Just as the life of the Church is strengthened through more frequent celebration of the Eucharistic mystery, similar we may hope for a new stimulus for the life of the Spirit from a growing reverence for the word of God, which "lasts forever" (Is. 40:8; see 1 Peter 1:23-25).

*T*his last paragraph of *Dei Verbum* explains that one of the most important duties of the bishops, is to provide good translations of the Bible with suitable introductions and notes. It could be argued that one of the reasons for the success of the Reformation in drawing whole countries away from the unity of the Catholic Church was that the bishops at that time were slow in providing good translations of the Scriptures into the vernacular. Thus, at the same time as the sixteenth century printing revolution began, the mass of Catholic people had only Latin versions of the Bible to read, or alternatively translations accompanied by hostile interpretations of the Scriptures by Luther in Germany or Tyndale in England. By the time the Douay Version came for English-speaking Catholics, the Reformation had already taken its hold on half of Europe.

Nowadays, there are dozens of good translations of the Bible, and, as we have said before, these translations often come with the full authority of the Catholic bishops together with leaders of other Christian denominations. It is one of the best examples of ecumenical co-operation. There is a quite bewildering choice of translations of the Bible to choose from. It is not for me to say which is the best translation. Just take your pick!

The penultimate paragraph, of *Dei Verbum* gives us a final challenge, a final twist if you like. It encourages the production of versions of the Bible to distribute among "non-Christians". Admittedly most of us Catholics do not think of the Bible as a means of evangelisation; but *Dei Verbum* does! A group of Evangelical businessmen

> [*Dei Verbum*]... encourages the production of versions of the Bible to distribute among "non-Christians".

"The best book to read is the Bible......."!

clubbed together to place a Bible in each hotel room These Gideon Bibles have become famous. Wha spiritual good might have been done for a lonel commercial traveller going to bed at night, just glancin at the Gideon Bible in his hotel room!

This thrust towards evangelisation is a most appropriat ending to *Dei Verbum*. We saw right at the beginnin that the Council Fathers did not just wish to defend th truth of divine revelation in this document. They wante to draw the whole Church into a greater awarenes of the purpose of divine revelation, which is to mak us sharers in the divine nature. But if, as recent Pope have emphasised again and again, the Church exists t evangelise, then the prime instrument of evangelisatio is the Bible itself, to draw more and more men an women of our time into that *koinónia*.

Thank you for your patient reading of my commentary which I hope will draw you more and more back to rea *Dei Verbum* itself. And remember of course, even more "The best book to read is the Bible......."!

A prayer when you begin the reading of scripture "Speak, Lord, your servant is listening". [1 Samuel 3:9] This is the response of the little boy Samuel, serving i the Temple, who heard the voice of YHWH calling hir by name during the night.

NOTES

Preface

Article 1:

1. cf. St. Augustine, "De Catechizandis Rudibus," C.IV 8: PL. 40, 316.

Chapter I

Article 2:

2. cf. Matt. 11:27; John 1:14 and 17; 14:6; 17:1-3; 2 Cor 3:16 and 4, 6; Eph. 1, 3-14.

Article 4:

3. Epistle to Diognetus, c. VII, 4: Funk, Apostolic Fathers, I, p. 403.

Article 5:

4. First Vatican Council, Dogmatic Constitution on the Catholic Faith, Chap. 3, "On Faith:" Denzinger 1789 (3008).

5. Second Council of Orange, Canon 7: Denzinger 180 (377); First Vatican Council, loc. cit.: Denzinger 1791 (3010).

Article 6:

6. First Vatican Council, Dogmatic Constitution on the Catholic Faith, Chap. 2, "On Revelation:" Denzinger 1786 (3005).

7. Ibid: Denzinger 1785 and 1786 (3004 and 3005).

Chapter II

Article 7:

1. cf. Matt. 28:19-20, and Mark 16:15; Council of Trent, session IV, Decree on Scriptural Canons: Denzinger 783 (1501).

2. cf. Council of Trent, loc. cit.; First Vatican Council, session III, Dogmatic Constitution on the Catholic Faith,

Chap. 2, "On revelation:" Denzinger 1787 (3005).

3. St. Irenaeus, "Against Heretics" III, 3, 1: PG 7, 848; Harvey, 2, p. 9.

Article 8:

4. cf. Second Council of Nicea: Denzinger 303 (602); Fourth Council of Constance, session X, Canon 1: Denzinger 336 (650-652).

5. cf. First Vatican Council, Dogmatic Constitution on the Catholic Faith, Chap. 4, "On Faith and Reason:" Denzinger 1800 (3020).

Article 9:

6. cf. Council of Trent, session IV, loc. cit.: Denzinger 783 (1501).

Article 10:

7. cf. Pius XII, apostolic constitution, "Munificentissimus Deus," Nov. 1, 1950: A.A.S. 42 (1950) p. 756; Collected Writings of St. Cyprian, Letter 66, 8: Hartel, III, B, p. 733: "The Church [is] people united with the priest and the pastor together with his flock."

8. cf. First Vatican Council, Dogmatic Constitution on the Catholic Faith, Chap. 3 "On Faith:" Denzinger 1792 (3011).

9. cf. Pius XII, encyclical "Humani Generis," Aug. 12, 1950: A.A.S. 42 (1950) pp. 568-69: Denzinger 2314 (3886).

Chapter III

Article 11:

1. cf. First Vatican Council, Dogmatic Constitution on the Catholic Faith, Chap. 2 "On Revelation:" Denzinger 1787 (3006); Biblical Commission, Decree of June 18,1915: Denzinger 2180 (3629): EB 420; Holy Office, Epistle of Dec. 22, 1923: EB 499.

2. cf. Pius XII, encyclical "Divino Afflante Spiritu," Sept 30, 1943: A.A.S. 35 (1943) p. 314; Enchiridion Bible (EB) 556.

3. "In" and "for" man: cf. Heb. 1, and 4, 7; ("in"): 2 Sm 23,2; Matt.1:22 and various places; ("for"): First Vatican Council, Schema on Catholic Doctrine, note 9: Col Lac. VII, 522.

4. Leo XIII, encyclical "Providentissimus Deus," Nov. 18 1893: Denzinger 1952 (3293); EB 125.

5. cf. St. Augustine, "Gen. ad Litt." 2, 9, 20:PL 34 270-271; Epistle 82, 3: PL 33, 277: CSEL 34, 2, p 354. St. Thomas, "On Truth," Q. 12, A. 2, C.Counc of Trent, session IV, Scriptural Canons: Denzinger 78? (1501). Leo XIII, encyclical "Providentissimus Deus:" EB 121, 124, 126-127. Pius XII, encyclical "Divino Afflante Spiritu:" EB 539.

Article 12:

6. St. Augustine, "City of God," XVII, 6, 2: PL 41, 537 CSEL. XL, 2, 228.

7. St. Augustine, "On Christian Doctrine" III, 18, 26; PL 34, 75-76.

8. Pius XII, loc. cit. Denziger 2294 (3829-3830); EB 557 562.

9. cf. Benedict XV, encyclical "Spiritus Paraclitus" Sept 15, 1920:EB 469. St. Jerome, "In Galatians' 5, 19-20 PL 26, 417 A.

10. cf. First Vatican Council, Dogmatic Constitution or the Catholic Faith, Chapter 2, "On Revelation:" Denziger 1788 (3007).

Article 13:

11. St. John Chrysostom "In Genesis" 3, 8 (Homily l7 1): PG 53, 134; "Attemperatio" [in English "Suitable

adjustment"] in Greek "synkatabasis."

Chapter IV
Article 15:
1. Pius XI, encyclical 'Mit Brennender Sorge," March 14, 1937: A.A.S. 29 (1937) p. 51.

Article 16:
2. St. Augustine, "Quest. in Hept." 2,73: PL 34,623.

3. St. Irenaeus, "Against Heretics" III, 21,3: PG 7,950; Same as 25,1: Harvey 2, p. 115). St. Cyril of Jerusalem, "Catech." 4,35; PG 33,497. Theodore of Mopsuestia, "In Soph." 1,4-6: PG 66, 452D-453A.

Chapter V
Article 18:
1. cf. St. Irenaeus, "Against Heretics" III, 11; 8: PG 7,885, Sagnard Edition, p. 194.

Article 19:
Due to the necessities of translation, footnote 2 follows footnote 3 in text of Article 19.)

2. cf. John 14:26; 16:13.

3. John 2:22; 12:16; cf. 14:26; 16:12-13; 7:39.

4. cf. instruction "Holy Mother Church" edited by Pontifical Consilium for Promotion of Bible Studies; A.A.S. 56 (1964) p. 715.

Chapter VI
Article 23:
1. cf. Pius XII, encyclical "Divino Afflante Spiritu:" EB 551, 553, 567. Pontifical Biblical Commission, Instruction on Proper Teaching of Sacred Scripture in Seminaries and Religious Colleges, May 13, 1950: A.A.S. 42 (1950) pp. 495-505.

2. cf. Pius XII, ibid: EB 569.

Article 24:

3. cf. Leo XIII, encyclical "Providentissmus Deus:" EB 114; Benedict XV, encyclical "Spiritus Paraclitus:" EB 483.

Article 25:

4. St. Augustine Sermons, 179,1: PL 38,966.

5. St. Jerome, Commentary on Isaiah, Prol.: PL 24,17 cf. Benedict XV, encyclical "Spiritus Paraclitus:" EB 475-480; Pius XII, encyclical "Divino Afflante Spiritu:" EB 544.

6. St. Ambrose, On the Duties of Ministers I, 20,88: PL I6,50.

7. St. Irenaeus, "Against Heretics" IV, 32,1: PG 7, 1071 (Same as 49,2) Harvey, 2, p. 255.